PATHWA~ ~O
POSITIVITY

KAMAL FERNANDEZ
on
Sports Dog Training

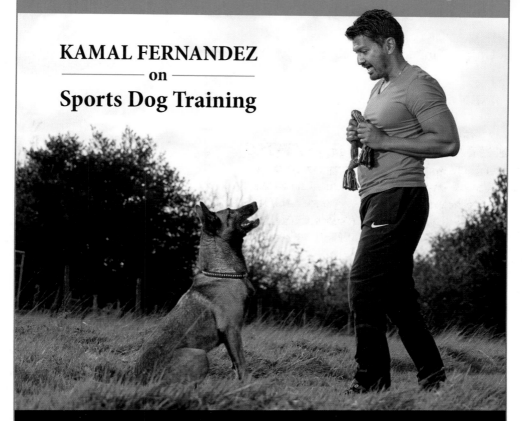

"Kamal is all about learning and growing" **SUSAN GARRETT**

First published in 2019 by First Stone
an imprint of Westline Publishing Limited
The Old Hen House,
St Martin's Farm,
Zeals,
Warminster,
BA12 6NZ,
United Kingdom

ISBN 9781 910488 52 2

Cover photo: Dylan Collard
Location photography: Becky Austin

Printed in Turkey by Printworks Global

0 1 2 3 4 5 6 7 8 9

Contents

Foreword by Susan Garrett   5

Introduction   7

Chapter One: FINDING THE PERFECT DOG   10
Plan A; Plan B; When things go wrong; 1. Lack of understanding; 2 Lack of
motivation; 3. Lack of boundaries; 4. Relationship issues; 5. Physical issues.

Chapter Two: THE POWER OF POSITIVE LEARNING   26
Positive reinforcement; Negative reinforcement; Negative punishment;
Positive punishment; Putting it into practice; Guide to reinforcement;
Annoyingly adolescent.

Chapter Three: HOW TO BE AN EFFECTIVE CLICKER TRAINER   37
My training journey; Getting started; My rules of clicker training; Shaping and
luring; The modern principles of shaping; Clicker positives; Clicker pitfalls;
The big four; Key to effective clicker training.

Chapter Four: DOES CLICKER TRAINING WORK FOR EVERY DOG?   53
How reinforcement works; Resistance to shaping; Learned helplessness;
Concept training; Reward specific markers.

Chapter Five: BUILDING PLAY   63
A voyage of discovery; Understanding play; Assessing your dog for tug; Those
that want to tug; Golden rules for establishing tug; Those that are reluctant to
tug; Jessie's story; Top tips for reluctant tuggers; Shaping play.

Chapter Six: DEFINING GOALS AND TEACHING NEW BEHAVIOURS   77
What are you looking for? Training toolbox; Making a plan; Pairing
behaviours; Putting behaviours on cue.

Chapter Seven: TO PUNISH OR NOT TO PUNISH?   84

What is punishment?; What are the options?; Time-out; Is punishment necessary? Punishment versus reinforcement.

Chapter Eight: COPING WITH STRESS AND FRUSTRATION   101

A better understanding; Practical measures.

Chapter Nine: REFINING REWARD AND REINFORCEMENT   105

Creating drive and desire; Hierarchy of reinforcement; Reinforcement zone; Transfer of value; Combining food and play; Ending on a good note.

Chapter Ten: CHAINING BEHAVIOURS   114

Starting the chain; Linking behaviours; Completing the chain; Proofing games; Have fun!

Chapter Eleven: CHANNELING DRIVE AND BUILDING DURATION   122

Key factors; You've got it – now make it last! Building duration step-by-step.

Chapter Twelve: MY FAVOURITE FOUNDATION GAMES   127

Basic skills; What treats should I use? Susan Garrett's *Itsyerchoice;* Saying "please"; Simon says; Hand touch; Spider hands; Collar grabs; Restrained recalls; Food circuits; Corner throws; Name game; Five for five; Around a cone; Value for a dead toy; Toy swaps; Out with it!; Building toy swaps into an IPR; Informal play retrieve; Summing up.

Appendix   160

Foreword

by Susan Garrett

I first met Kamal more than 10 years ago when I was teaching a dog training workshop in the UK. I remember him as the guy who asked a lot of great questions.

Fast forward to 2015 and it was confirmed for me he had a different approach in life. You see he was sitting opposite me as I had just started to interview him as a guest for my high level mastermind dog training group. Within 5 minutes Kamal had turned the tables and he ended up interviewing me!

Here was an up and coming dog trainer with an amazing opportunity to share his story with a focused group of dog trainers and he chose instead to turn the spotlight back on me. It is something very few, maybe no other elite "achiever" in life would do. Most people love to talk about themselves, elite performers in any walk of life maybe more so. Dog trainers are no exception, but here Kamal was passing up this rare opportunity to do just that.

The first question that may spring to your mind would be "why?" Why did he turn the tables on such an opportunity? However, as you will learn by reading *Pathway to Positivity,* the "why" of behaviour is rarely important.

Too often dog owners seek to question "why" does my dog do THAT! The truth is none of us will ever know the answer to such a question for certain. Only the dog will know "why" he chose to dig up your flower bed, or pee on the sofa or chew that particular pair of winter gloves. And, in just the same way as Kamal turned the tables on that interview, the why isn't as important as the what and the how.

As Kamal so beautifully demonstrates in *Pathway to Positivity* the only way to change behaviour is to describe what you want to see happen, observe what you now have happening and create a plan that plots your steps to go from point A to point B. The why is not the issue; the issue is the WHAT followed by the HOW.

Susan Garrett: World renowned dog trainer and behaviourist, international agility competitor and instructor.

What do you have, what do you want, and how are you going to get it. Through his training stories Kamal shares those steps of how he gets from point A to point B with a variety of different dogs.

Through *Pathway to Positivity* Kamal shares his discoveries as he interprets the science of behaviour on his journey of helping dogs to learn.

It is an ongoing journey of progress and discovery. It is about how one man sorts through the sometimes complex science of behaviour, to come up with ways to break through to seemingly unreachable dogs. His engaging anecdotes are sure to inspire you, and it is very likely you will be able to see the behaviour of your own dog in one of Kamal's.

As I reflect back to 2015 sitting opposite Kamal I realise the "what" of that situation was that by asking me the questions, he opened up the potential to learn for himself. He wasn't interested in being interviewed because Kamal is all about learning and growing, and growth in life comes from asking not telling. This is the philosophy you will be learning as you read through his book. "Telling" has the potential to create opposition in others, whereas "asking" has the potential to open communication and deepen relationships.

This is a key to success in dog training. "Telling" your dog has the potential to create opposition whereas "asking" gives you an opportunity to evaluate what your dog has learned and alter things if the outcome isn't what you were wanting. Asking is deepening that relationship you have with your dog.

As you journey into the world of reinforcement-based dog training, you will see how the best results come from asking the best questions. This is the place where the learning organically occurs in both the dog and the trainer. This is where training becomes learning to ask better questions. This is what *Pathway to Positivity* will give you – insight into how the best dog trainers ask the best questions. It is a guide for you to be able to start asking those better questions, both of yourself and of your dog.

Introduction

L et me start by thanking you! That's right, I want to say thank you! I am one of those privileged people who gets to live out his dream, and follow his passion, every day. That's because people like you take the time to see, hear – and now read about – what I do. It's a true blessing, which I will never take for granted.

The reason I can say this with so much conviction is because the path that I now follow has come from nowhere. With my background, the chances of becoming a successful dog trainer were almost non-existent.

When you read the stories of other dog trainers, their journey generally starts with early interactions with dogs or animals.

But for me, there was none of this. My family were not 'doggy' or even 'animally' for that matter. In fact, they don't really like dogs or other animals. I was brought up in a household, and in a culture, where animals were not seen as pets or companions. But from the earliest age I had a

My passion for dogs started at a young age.

deep love for all dogs. My father didn't read me stories; I insisted that he read me books on dog breeds. Before I ever even owned a dog, I knew every breed, and could tell you their history, purpose and role.

I was – and still am – obsessed with dogs. I love them; I love everything about them. But above all, I love what they have given me and what they have taught me.

By nature I am not a patient person; nothing holds my focus or attention for long. I have a thousand thoughts constantly in my mind, yet, when I have a dog in front of me, everything becomes about that being. I can empathise with a dog naturally; I have infinite patience with him, even though I am the world's least patient person – and I adore them all – big, small, fat, thin, hairy, smooth, black, white or yellow…

But, for me, it is not enough to love and understand dogs – I want to make their world a better place. My work is concerned with finding a method of training and a way of communicating that will be effective for all dogs – from the family pet to the top-class competitor.

My journey to becoming a reinforcement-based dog trainer, has been epic. I have learnt so much, both from the dogs that I have worked with and the handlers I have helped. I have moved from viewing dog training in black and white to seeing it in high definition colour. I cannot and would not train a dog any other way.

My students have competed at national, international and world championship level in obedience, working trials, agility, and canine freestyle. However, I am equally proud of the many pet dogs I have worked with. To see a dog reach his true potential, in any sphere, is the ultimate reward.

In this book, I am sharing my method of training in the hope that you can make your dog's life better. If you can introduce clarity, understanding and compassion when you are communicating with your dog, my work is done.

There are many I would like to thank for their help and support:

The teachers who have guided me, steered me and shaped me to be the trainer and person I am… Each has shared with me their expertise, knowledge and perspective but, above all, their passion. I consider myself privileged to see truly 'great' dog men and women in their homes, in their element, interacting and training their dogs. I am still in awe of your brilliance and the gift you have shared with me.

My family and my friends – those in my extended family who have taken this journey with me, often blindly and without total understanding, yet always with love, support and belief. Those in my 'circle' know who they are, and they know the place they hold in my heart; you have been there when I needed you most, before the journey even began. Having someone in your corner that truly believes in you, is a heartwarming gift. I am eternally grateful to you all.

My dogs, past, present and future – they are, by far, my greatest teachers. They have pulled me through the dark times, and put me in the light. I love you all, each one so unique. You have pushed me, challenged me and indulged me. Without them, I would be just existing – but with them I get to fly.

Competing with my Malinois, Thriller. I have learnt so much on my journey to positive reinforcement dog training. *Photo: Brian McGovern*

Finally, my Neave and Nailah. This book is a lesson to you both. Follow your heart, find your passion and live a life of joy and happiness as a result of it. I can wish for nothing better for you both. Reach for the stars – they are closer than you think.

Chapter One

FINDING THE PERFECT DOG

I am ready to get a new dog, and I have made a few decisions about it. I say 'it' as I haven't decided on the breed or gender, or even where 'it' is coming from. So I welcome any suggestions people can make...

PLAN A

Firstly, my priority is that this dog loves to work! I am mainly getting this dog for a sport; I haven't decided which one exactly, but I shall definitely do something with 'it'. 'It' has to have that 'can do' attitude and 'it' has to absolutely love interacting with me. 'It' has to be totally focused on me, no matter what is going on, and 'it' has to have an amazing temperament in all situations. To be honest, I'm getting too long in the tooth to fix dogs, so 'it' has to be 100 per cent sound, and 'it' has to be an amazing pet. My dogs are part of the family, and with a young child, 'it' has to be easy to live with.

'It' also has to be dog friendly. I have dogs in for training constantly and I have my own dogs, so 'it' has to be super friendly. But not weak with other dogs – I don't want 'it' to get bullied.

'It' also has to have amazing structure; as I want a performance dog this is a top priority. 'It' has to be an athlete. 'It' has to have great play drive and great food drive – ideally in equal measure – so I can use both without conflict.

There is so much to consider when you go in search of the perfect dog.

'It' has to have a really sound temperament in all environments. I travel a lot for work and may take this dog abroad, so I need 'it' to accept this, warts and all. 'It' needs to be friendly and adaptable, but I don't want 'it' to be into anyone else but me. This is massively important for a working dog, or even a pet dog. There should never be a moment when my dog prefers anyone else, or is distracted by any other thing – the focus must always be on me.

As previously mentioned, I'm not sure what sport I'll do, but 'it' has to be able to jump correctly. 'It' needs the correct conformation to jump effortlessly and save 'its' body. I want to have a long career with this dog, as I have had to retire dogs prematurely due to physical issues, so this dog definitely has to be sound in that department.

'It' also has to have great structure for obedience. I want 'it' to have the physical ability to assume an upright position and move in a flamboyant manner – but 'its' bum needs to be straight, and 'its' topline must be level.

'It' may also do bite-work, so I want that edge that is needed for dynamic and

Thriller with my daughter, Neave.

explosive bites – but not too much, or control may be an issue.

'It' needs sufficient strength to take a challenge or re-attack, but to be calm with my daughter, Neave, and anyone that comes to our home. 'It' cannot show any aggression – that's a definite. It cannot show aggression to any dog, person, animal or thing, ever.

'It' has to love to run and chase. Both of these are needed for what I plan to do – but not too much. Neave moves quickly and I don't want this to trigger a chase and bite response. As my free time is getting less and less; the most I can walk is 30 minutes a day – so then 'it' must be able to chill at home. 'It' has to be biddable so 'it' doesn't object to being handled by me, or anyone else, including a vet who may need to give a detailed hands-on examination.

'It' also has to be clever. I want 'it' to do multiple sports and I want to get

'it' trained as quickly as possible. 'It' has to be bright – but not so intelligent as to be unco-operative.

'It' has to love repetition. A lot of training is repetitive so 'it' has to thrive on this – but I don't want 'it' to be obsessive. I don't have time to train every day, so 'it' needs to accept that and have an off switch.

'It' has to be able to live in the house and be well-behaved. I don't like dogs on furniture, or dogs that jump up, or dogs that go out of doors before me. So 'it' has to be nice to live with.

'It' also has to have a coat. In obedience, a really short-coated dog may show a gap on my leg, and I may get marked for it. But I don't like dog hair everywhere, so 'it' can't have too much hair. 'It' also has to have nice, even markings and a good colour. I like dogs that are unique and stand out as being 'different'. I think that makes for a better picture, and makes us more eye-catching.

And finally, I may have a litter from 'it'. So 'it' can't be spayed/castrated – but I don't want 'it' to have any hormone issues. Bitches can go off work with seasons and dogs can be distracted by bitches. I definitely don't want any of that – but I want a pup from 'it' in the future so neutering isn't an option.

Anyone got any ideas about where I could find 'it'? If you are looking to the sky at this point, you may not be far wrong!

Or I do have a Plan B...

PLAN B

Get a dog I like, love it, train it and accept it. Work with what I've got. Be a dog trainer and dog lover. Full stop. As a professional trainer of both performance and companion dogs, I have conversations about the search for 'it' on a regular basis.

I get numerous emails and calls from people outlining all the things they need, or don't need, and I truly sympathise. I want to be able to help.

The list of expectations we have for our dogs is huge. And often we forget how un-dog like we are asking an individual to be. Don't chew the furniture that smells like meat, don't chase the small, furry thing that runs fast (it happens to be the neighbour's cat...), don't bite the strange dog that tries to invade your personal space, don't bite the man that comes to the door to deliver stuff, even though you don't know him, have never met him and he's wearing a strange hat.

Personality traits are all interlinked. Fear is linked to aggression, aggression is linked to prey drive, prey drive and herding instinct are twin components, and a biddable temperament is linked to submissiveness.

So when you look for a dog to have a certain quality, the chances of finding one where the needle falls at exactly the right spot on each personality trait is nearly impossible.

The key is to find the dog that suits you. To adapt and be a better dog trainer,

Perfection does not exist, so you learn to train the dog in front of you.

not just someone that can train a certain type. So your perfect dog probably isn't perfect, but rather he is perfect for you – and that's the secret.

I bred a litter of pups and each one of the pups went to close friends who would tell me, honestly, what they thought of their new charges. Without exception, every owner was delighted with what they got – every puppy was adored. How can that be? Did all of them get a perfect puppy? Obviously, because they were bred from my two perfect dogs...

Of course I believe that, but leaving my natural prejudices aside, what really happened? The perfect matches came about because we had detailed discussions about the pup that each person wanted, and what I thought would suit them best. So the pup they chose was a collaborative decision and, as such, each one has turned out to be perfect. The puppies match the people who chose them. If they had chosen differently, it may not have been quite so perfect.

It is also important to bear in mind that having belief in your dog will set you on the road to perfection. The puppies I bred were not all angels – but from day one, they were perceived as being perfect. They were perfect when they wouldn't sleep through the night, when they were car sick and when they didn't tug at first. They were perfect tearing through tunnels, leaping over

14

jumps and sleeping on the bed. Every one of us is looking for someone that sees us as perfect. Dogs are no different. See them as perfect, and they just might be.

WHEN THINGS GO WRONG

Building a relationship – whether it be with a dog or a fellow human being – should always be based on positives. What is it you like? What is funny or interesting? What is unusual? What do you want to discover?

A positive attitude breeds success. It sees opportunities, it embraces learning – it is a way of thinking that makes everything possible. In contrast, a negative attitude adopts failure as the inevitable outcome. The challenges are too difficult, the journey is too frustrating, and there is no hope of change.

What attitude do you want to adopt when training your dog? It is a no-brainer; positive training and reinforcement is the only way forward. So why is it that so many dog owners are preoccupied with identifying their dogs' problems?

• Why doesn't my dog come back when I call?
• Why doesn't my dog like to tug?
• Why does my dog break his stays?

The list is endless.

My training method is entirely based on positive reinforcement (as outlined in Chapter Two: The Power of Positive Learning). However, before we can embrace this full on, we first need to lose the doubts and the negativity.

In my experience, there are five core reasons why dogs don't do as we ask:
1. Lack of understanding
2. Lack of motivation
3. Lack of boundaries
4. Relationship issues
5. Physical issues

If you can identify which one is applicable – and work on it – you will be on the road to becoming a positive dog trainer, and enjoying all the benefits that will bring.

It could be that your dog simply does not understand what you want him to do.

1. LACK OF UNDERSTANDING

When you have taught your dog a behaviour, are you sure that he understands it? If you have taken the time and trouble to teach an exercise, of course he knows what to do. But how sure are you? Do you want to place a bet – £1,000 on your dog performing the behaviour correctly?

Oh, well… if the sun is shining, and the wind is in the right direction… Now the doubts and the hesitancy creep in. But if you can state, with complete confidence, that your dog knows the behaviour you are training, you are on to a winner. It is not simply proof that he knows an exercise, it is proof that you are communicating with him effectively. This is the foundation for all that you may achieve with your pet dog, or with your sports competitor. In fact, it lies at the crux of your relationship.

If you are an experienced trainer, it may be humbling to admit that you are not getting through to your dog; if you are a novice owner, you may feel daunted by the task ahead. However, if you can be 100 per cent honest about your dog's level of understanding, it will ultimately help you to achieve more.

When you step into the competition ring – or when you are free-running your dog in the park – you need self-belief. Regardless of whether you are asking your dog to perform a complex task under the pressure of competition, or a straightforward recall in the park, you need the knowledge that your dog can do it. Of course, dogs are dogs and they may make mistakes. And that's fine, but you don't want it to be because of your shortcomings in teaching. You want to stand proudly with an inner confidence in your dog's ability.

To create understanding, there are two processes you must incorporate into your training: generalising and proofing.

GENERALISING

I have lost count of the number of times I have heard someone say: "...but he always does it at home..."

That may well be the case, but have you taught him to perform the behaviour in different locations? A dog's brain differs from others in the fact that he does not generalise. Just because he has performed a behaviour at home, does not mean that he can apply the learning when he is a different situation. 'Generalisation' is the technical term for explaining to your dog that the rules for earning rewards still apply, regardless of the situation or environment.

It means taking your training to lots of different locations, and teaching your dog that the rules and criteria, in relation to that behaviour, are applicable in any location, at any time.

PROOFING

This is the term used for the process of making your dog 100 per cent foolproof when he performs an exercise. Proofing occurs at two distinct points in a training programme.

The first stage is when the dog has learnt an exercise in one situation, and you need to test his ability to perform it in any environment. A better term for this stage would be 'generalising'. You are getting the dog to 'generalise' performing an activity in any situation, regardless of distractions.

The second distinct stage occurs once an exercise is taught and repeated several hundred, if not thousands, of times – at which point your dog is close to understanding the task! Now you alter the exercise slightly and ask the dog to perform the behaviour, regardless of the variation introduced. For example, you set you dog up at an angle for a sendaway, and ask him to correct himself.

17

This stage can be time consuming and cause confusion in the dog's mind. Don't panic! This is absolutely normal and to be expected. It shows the dog is trying to understand. Be consistent and make sure you alter only one thing at a time. Proofing is not easy; it can make some dogs anxious, some get wound up, and others feel like quitting. Just persevere – making sure you keep the learning experience positive – because the outcome will be a dog that has far more depth to his knowledge, and will be ready for any situation that a show, or any other environment, can present.

LUMPERS VERSUS SPLITTERS

It is important to bear in mind that the logical sequence we can see in an exercise, such as a retrieve, is meaningless as far as a dog is concerned. We therefore need to split the exercise into bite-sized chunks and feed these tiny pieces of information to our dogs. This is what effective clicker training is all about (see Chapter Three).

Traditional training, which involves lumping together a number of behaviours, may seem like a sensible shortcut to us, but it can easily result in muddle and confusion. So, as a trainer, choosing to be a 'lumper' or a 'splitter' can have a big impact on your teaching – and on the likely outcome.

Every exercise you teach your dog can be broken down into numerous pieces. For example, listed below are the 27 component parts required for a competition retrieve. Each part needs to be taught, polished and rewarded:
• Drive for article
• Grip
• Grip with duration
• Proofing grip
• Orientating to heelwork position
• Orientating to heelwork position with sit
• Sit, wait
• Look
• Look with duration
• Look with duration and proofed
• Sit, wait and look
• Sit, wait and look with duration

- Sit, wait and look with duration, article thrown
- Marking as article falls
- Outrun
- Pick-up off floor
- Pick-up
- Return
- Present
- Angle present
- Left hand pick-up
- Right hand pick-up
- Distance
- Different articles
- Present with duration
- Finish
- Sit at heel

The biggest difference between traditional training and clicker training is based on this decision.... do I lump or do I split?

Taking the example of a retrieve, lumping – which involves lumping large sections of the exercise together into one mass of information – would mean holding the dog's collar, throwing the article, sending the dog to collect it, then calling him into a present. You have 'lumped' the exercises together in the hope that the dog learns the intricacy of each component.

A splitter will break the exercise down into tiny pieces and teach each part separately. Each segment is generalised and proofed, before piecing it back together again. This may take time but, ultimately, it leads to stronger behaviour and a better understanding. It also means that the behaviour is more likely to withstand the rigours of competing, or any other pressurised or challenging situation.

2. LACK OF MOTIVATION

Motivation comes in many forms, and what constitutes reward and reinforcement for one dog may not be appropriate for another. It could be that what your dog finds rewarding in one environment won't cut the mustard in another.

Play is all about finding something your dog values.

Ideally, a dog would have equal value for toys and food – but this is rarely, if ever, the case. Most dogs have a preference. The key is to create value for all items that you wish to use within your training. With some dogs this does not always mean the obvious choices.

This is where the Premack principle will assist you. This theory of reinforcement, devised by American psychologist, David Premack, states that more probable behaviours will reinforce less probable behaviours. In practical terms, this means that you can use an activity your dog really enjoys to reinforce a behaviour he finds mundane. So, for example, you can reinforce the stay exercise with a game of tug.

Some of my dogs have shown a liking for abstract items, or developed fetishes that I have used to build value for things that they previously found boring. I have had dogs that would chase the hosepipe or sprinkler, and I have used that to build value for tug toys or even food. One of my dogs had an obsession with plastic bags, so I harnessed it to build tug drive. I would wrap a plastic bag into a slim sausage-shaped roll, almost like a plastic bite bar, and use it to reinforce her for tugging.

Play has been around for as long as dogs have existed – they invented it. Although play has various forms and technical terms to encompass it (positive reinforcement, building drive, etc.), it still is exactly that – play! So how do you play with a dog in a constructive manner that will develop instinct and build his confidence and self-esteem?

Dogs are, by nature, predators – even that little Poodle who scarcely stirs from the sofa is a highly capable predator. Ok, he may not be a killer, but he has the instinct. A dog's physiological and psychological make-up allows him to be effective at what he needs to do to survive, and, going back in time, that meant hunting.

By imitating prey and mimicking dogs interacting with prey, we cement the social bond between us, similar to the way a pack of wolves would behave. Through this, we can build a dog's desire to interact with us and therefore to work with us. Changing body posture, physical contact, eye contact, sound and choice of toy can all have an effect on a dog's attitude and motivation. It then becomes a matter of how we use this understanding in our dog-handler interactions to influence the end product.

3. LACK OF BOUNDARIES

This is an issue that can be contentious; surely the way we live with our dogs is a matter of personal preference? However, those of us that choose to train our dogs using reinforcement, need to embrace the mantra devised by world-renowned dog trainer, Susan Garrett: "positive is not permissive".

My dogs have rules and boundaries, and it is these rules and boundaries that allow me to create clarity. Just ask yourself the question: "Is my dog a lager lout or a gentlemen?"

Investing in your dog's day-to-day domestic life is crucial if you are to have a relationship where he is an asset to your life, and not a hindrance. The biggest investment you can make is training the recall. Susan Garrett says: "A recall is a reflection of the relationship you have with your dog" – and never a truer word was spoken.

4. RELATIONSHIP ISSUES

When you have considered all the other factors that affect your training, and yet you can't quite put your finger on what the issue is, it could be something to do with the relationship you have with your dog.

Dogs live in the present, and the key is to accept them for what they are. I would love to be able to say that I had an instant rapport with every dog I have owned. I would love to say that I was smitten right from the start. I have had that experience with most of my dogs – but there are a few where it took a little longer. That's right, my name is Kamal Fernandez, and I didn't have an instant head-over-heels, fall in love feeling when I saw some of my dogs – I admit it! What a bad owner/dog lover that makes me!

But I know some of the people reading this will have felt exactly the same.

We all want to have that instantaneous connection with a pup/rescue dog – that gut wrenching, skip-a-heartbeat feeling. This is when you know, that no matter what your pup does or how he turns out, you will love him, accept him, and adore him. Yes, he may have some little quirks; yes, he may have some hang-ups, but despite that…you love him. Warts and all.

But sometimes, that just doesn't happen. Sorry to burst the Disney bubble of happy ever after, but sometimes it takes work. There are several examples of relationship issues that I see and have experienced myself, but the two I come across most frequently are second dog syndrome, and what I call, 'mismatch of personalities'.

SECOND DOG SYNDROME (SDS)

This occurs when you have had one dog, a particularly special dog that you just clicked with. You instantly had that head-over-heels feeling when you saw that dog, and he just seemed to know what you wanted or, with minimal training picked up stuff and made your dreams come true, while being a great family pet.

When the time comes to find another dog, the new dog will never meet the expectations set by the first. You will have had a connection to the first dog, which makes it all the more challenging to see this new dog as an individual and accept him for what he is, rather than living in the shadow of your previous dog. So no matter what he does, he will never measure up.

You may not get what you expect – but there is so much to learn along the way.

Labelling your dog as 'stupid', 'difficult' or 'untrainable' will create a self-fulfilling prophecy – and you will find that this is what people feed back to you.

The first dog is your equivalent of Rin Tin Tin, and your second dog, is just a normal dog that does normal dog things. Often, the reality is that your first 'dream' dog was that way despite you, not because of you. Your second dog will make you a dog trainer. In a lifetime, you will get far more normal dogs then Rin Tin Tins.

MISMATCH OF PERSONALITIES

This variation on relationship issues is more common in dog sports. Often, people will get a breed of dog, or a type of dog, that they think will bring them success in their chosen discipline. However, the traits that make the dog so great for a particular sport can, equally, become a source of frustration and despair. The high-energy, full-on workaholic doesn't always clock off when you leave the competition setting. That OCD desire to 'do' is still there at 10pm, after a long day when all you want to do is chill out and relax!

It may be that a particular breed, breed type, or a particular personality, simply doesn't fit with who you are as a person, or doesn't suit your lifestyle. This can happen when people have the 'pick of a litter'. It has always baffled me when people talk about the pick of a litter.... pick for whom? One man's meat is another man's poison.

Or take the case of someone who adopts a rescue dog, and lives in the headspace where their dog is always a rescue case, rather than living in the now. I can say this from experience; I have had rescue dogs – several of them – and I have had a number of rehomed dogs, too. But once I took them on, they were no longer 'rescue' dogs; they are just 'my' dogs. When a rescued or rehomed dog first comes into my home, I give him a bath. For me, this is cathartic. I am washing away his past – and whatever issues he has – and from that moment onwards, I am focusing on solutions. What do I have, and what do I want? The bit in-between is simply dog training.

MAKING IT WORK

No one said relationships are easy, and in my time, I have experienced relationship issues with a number of my dogs. I have found myself telling anyone that will listen about the inadequacies of a particular dog, whilst inside I am comparing him to my previous dogs. I have found myself out-dogged, under-estimating what I had on my hands. I have had the 'rescue' dog whose every shortcoming was hung on that label, rather then taking ownership and acknowledging the part I had to play.

You might ask: why didn't I just find a nice home where the dog would have been loved and adored from the word go? Sometimes this is probably better for the dog. But for me, personally, I know that life is about lessons. The dog in front of me is there for a reason; he's there to teach me something. I may have to wait to see where that lesson falls into place, but it always will.

Perseverance, understanding, adapting, compromise, and acceptance – these are just a few of the life lessons my dogs have taught me. That's the choice I make; I don't judge people for the decisions they make. To each, his own. You don't always get what you want, you get what you need – whether you think you need it or not.

I have stuck with each and every one of my dogs and they have taught me some of the greatest lessons of my dog-training career. They have all ended up confident, well-adjusted and happy. I have developed a relationship that was based on truth, acceptance, mutual respect and admiration. I set ego aside. I removed all labels, and worked with what I had. I learnt to love each dog for who they were rather than what I wanted them to be, and then moulded them to the best they could be.

We compromised, we managed, we trained, we cried, we laughed, we contemplated giving up, we got frustrated and sometimes we didn't even like each other. At the end of it all, it was worth every struggle, every heartache and every challenge.

That's right, relationships take work! Relationships take work to create and nurture, to build a solid foundation that will stand the test of time. Any relationship is a long-term investment; you simply need to do the work.

5. PHYSICAL ISSUES

The final reason why dogs don't do as we ask, need or want, may be a physical issue. This could be a physical discomfort or pain, or a physical limitation.

I am fanatical about exercising my dogs and, being a hyperactive person, this is as much for my benefit as for the dogs'. However, it also means that they are more able to do the things that I ask, and perform them in the way that I would want. Speed, power, energy and drive come with a level of physical fitness. This would include co-ordination, flexibility, muscle strength and cardiovascular strength.

The other aspect of physicality is being aware of your dog's physical limitations. Selecting the dog, and breed, that has the physical ability to do what you require will alleviate any frustration further down the line. This may mean physical attributes, or capability. If your goal is to win the World Agility Championships, it may be wise to select a dog, or breed of dog, that has the ability to do the task.

Chapter Two

THE POWER OF
POSITIVE LEARNING

Imagine owning a dog that relished the idea or even the prospect of training? One for which the opportunity to learn a new exercise would send him into euphoria, or a dog that salivated at the chance of doing a 15 minute down stay in the rain?

Does this all seem a million miles away? Not with the power of reinforcement!

Most people are familiar with clicker training (see Chapter Three), or to give it its posh name, operant conditioning. The growing understanding of this methodology has allowed us to train elephants to do pirouettes and llamas to tap dance. However, I can't quite imagine elephants doing canine freestyle – especially not in lycra... But now the possibility of training a dog, regardless of breed, to do a series of exercises with verve and style is far more achievable.

Clicker training is not new. The chances are that you have been doing it for years. It's more about your approach to training which, in order to be successful, must rely on good timing, want, drive, clarity and understanding. You don't have to use a clicker to 'clicker train'; in fact, a clicker is such a specific tool you need the timing and precision of a brain

The joy of working with a dog who loves to learn!

surgeon to be really effective. But you do need to adopt the clicker trainer's reinforcement mantra: reinforcement builds behaviour. You only have to see how quickly a dog will learn a task if it is split into small steps and reinforced, rather than being lumped together in one big wedge of information (see Lumpers versus Splitters, page 18).

The power of positive reinforcement cannot be over-estimated. I know from personal experience that reinforcement is the only way to go when training your dogs for any competitive dog sport, and when you want to get the best from your companion dog. Make the task easy to achieve, yet challenging enough to engage the dog's brain. Remember, the more you play with your dog's brain, the more brain you'll have to play with!

To understand learning more fully, here is an overview of its four quadrants:

1. POSITIVE REINFORCEMENT

This is possibly the easiest, most effective consequence for a trainer to control (and easiest to understand, too!). Positive reinforcement means starting or adding something good, something your dog likes or enjoys. Because he wants to gain that good thing again, he will repeat the behaviour that seems to bring about that consequence.

Here are some examples of positive reinforcement:

- A worker gets a pay cheque for working.
- A dog gets a piece of liver for returning when called.
- A cat gets comfort for sleeping on the bed.
- A wolf gets a meal for hunting a deer.
- A child gets dessert for eating vegetables.
- A dog gets attention from his people when he barks.
- A child gets ice cream for begging incessantly.
- A toddler gets picked up and comforted for screaming.
- A dog gets to play in the park for pulling his owner there.
- A snacker gets a candy bar for putting money in the machine.

2. NEGATIVE REINFORCEMENT

Negative reinforcement increases a behaviour by ending, or taking away, something bad or aversive. By making your dog's circumstances better, you are rewarding him and increasing the likelihood that he will repeat the behaviour that was occurring when you ended the bad thing.

In order to use negative reinforcement, the trainer must be able to control the bad thing that is being taken away. This often means that the trainer must apply the bad thing, and, applying a bad thing might reduce whatever behaviour was going on at the time it was applied.

Reducing a behaviour by applying a bad thing is positive punishment. So when you apply the bad thing that you are going to use as a negative reinforcer, you run the risk of punishing some other behaviour.

One of the major results of taking away something bad is relief. So another way to think of negative reinforcement is that you are providing relief to your dog. But, of course, this makes it an example of positive reinforcement as you are providing something good, i.e. relief. Confused? Take a look at the following examples of negative reinforcement:

- A choke collar is loosened when the dog moves closer to the trainer.
- An ear pinch stops when the dog takes the dumbbell.
- Reins are loosened when a horse slows down.
- A car buzzer turns off when you put on your seat belt.
- Dad continues driving towards Disneyland when the kids are quiet.
- The hostage is released when the ransom is paid.
- Torture stops when the victim confesses.
- The baby stops crying when his mother feeds him.

3. POSITIVE PUNISHMENT

Positive punishment is something that is applied to reduce a behaviour. The term 'positive' can be confusing because, in common terms, 'positive' means something good, upbeat, happy, pleasant or rewarding.

Remember, this is technical terminology we are using so, in this context, 'positive' means added or 'started'. Also, bear in mind that in these terms, it is not the animal that is punished (treated badly to pay for some moral wrong), but the behaviour that is punished (in other words, reduced).

Our society seems to have a great fondness for positive punishment, in spite of all the problems associated with it. Here are some examples:

- A puppy peeing on the rug is punished with a swat by a newspaper.
- A dog's barking is punished with a startling squirt of citronella.
- A driver's speeding results in a ticket and fine.
- A baby's hand is burned when he touches the hot stove.
- Walking straight through low doorways is punished with a bonk on the head.

In all of these cases, the consequence (the positive punishment) reduces the behaviour's future occurrence.

4. NEGATIVE PUNISHMENT

Negative punishment relies on reducing behaviour by taking away something good. If your dog was enjoying or depending on something good, he will work to avoid having it taken away. He is less likely to repeat a behaviour that results in the loss of a good thing. This type of consequence is a little harder to control as you will see in the following examples:

Guide to Reinforcement

Here are some key points for those who want to live a life filled with reinforcement, yet want to have a dog that is social, obedient and a joy to own:

• Reinforce all the behaviours that you like, and want. Don't take it for granted that a dog who doesn't chew the furniture, will always choose not to do so. Ensure that you reinforce his decision to chew the toys you provide, even if it's just by praising or by making those items appealing. Train and teach the behaviours that you want, ensuring they have value for your dog. He has to benefit from his co-operation in some way.

• Manage the environment so that your dog doesn't have the opportunity to rehearse inappropriate behaviours. Limiting your dog's options to make mistakes is far smarter – and better dog training – then allowing him to access them in the first place. Equate your dog to a young child. You wouldn't allow a toddler to have unsolicited freedom as he/she wouldn't be able to make the appropriate choice when faced with temptation or uncertainty.

Adolescence is a particularly challenging time irrespective of the species! So prepare for, and anticipate this. See Annoyingly adolescent, page 33.

• A boy has his crayons taken away for fighting with his sister.
• The window looking into the neighbouring monkey's enclosure is shut when the monkey bites the trainer.
• The dog is put on the leash and taken from the park for coming to the owner when called (this causes the unintentional result of the dog being less likely to respond to the recall in the future).
• A teenager is grounded for misbehaviour.
• A dolphin trainer walks away with the fish bucket when the dolphin acts aggressively.

- Xena, the warrior princess, cuts off the arm of an opponent who refuses to tell her what she wants!

PUTTING IT INTO PRACTICE

The path I have followed to positive reinforcement based training hasn't been direct or smooth, but I wouldn't change a single step. I say this without judgment as to how others choose to train their dogs, but I wouldn't want to take any other journey.

I look back at the dogs I had early in my career, and I can only say what amazing dogs they were to put up with my poor communication and conflicting messages, and, somehow, still managed to work out what I wanted. In contrast, the dogs I train today have no such difficulties; the information they receive is so salient and clear. I can have a conversation with them and they can respond. They are neither silent, nor powerless, in the process.

Reinforcement based approaches to learning empower the student. It allows the dog to make a choice, and my role is to make my option the more appealing one. This creates a dog that sees life and decisions as games, and challenges and hurdles as opportunities to demonstrate their brilliance.

Imagine you were so full of confidence that, no matter what was thrown at you, you had the self-belief to complete the task. If you had the knowledge that nothing bad would happen, there would be no need to feel apprehensive or anxious, and if you were worried or confused, you knew that you would always be supported and empowered.

In this scenario, you are set up to succeed. You become the eternal optimist in the knowledge that you can deal with any setback. This is how my dogs perceive the world.

They are all confident, well-adjusted and joyful. They love to be alive, learn and and engage. This may not be how they start out, but as a result of the way they are reared and trained, it is the way they end up.

I still have boundaries with my dogs; I believe that this creates clarity and understanding which allows them to lead happy and fulfilling lives. However, I build this clarity and understanding by reinforcing choices, and value, for what I want the dog to do. I make this choice so favourable that the dog almost doesn't want to rehearse the incorrect choice. I then, systematically, test this choice. I see if I can tempt the dog to make errors, and then control the reinforcement this incorrect choice provides. This, in itself, deals with a vast array of issues that a dog will present to you.

For example, my dogs are all expected to come when called and remain in a controlled position until I give them permission to move. This means that with these simple behaviours, I can have control and, in turn, allow them lots of freedom. However, both these things are taught in stages, starting very simply and then increasing the challenge. When I start teaching a recall, I do so in an environment with minimal distraction. But as learning is established, I increase the challenge so that my dog can cope with any distraction he is faced with.

Being aware of what you are reinforcing is crucial for improving, changing and altering behaviour. An understanding of the four quadrants of reinforcement – positive and negative reinforcement and positive and negative punishment – is the bedrock on which all your training will be built. Everything you do from this point onwards will be built on this initial understanding.

I still have boundaries with my dogs as this gives them clarity as to how they should behave.

ANNOYINGLY ADOLESCENT!

There is a point in your dog's life when you may find him, at best, a little mischievous and, at worst, down right horrid! Yes that's right, even me, an avid dog lover, goes through a testing phase with most of my dogs, when I wonder if it's too late to give up dog training and get Koi Carp!

Between the ages of 6-14 months, your dog will enter into adolescence and, with it, you will most definitely face some challenges. This tends to happen just when you want to really progress your training, and start some of the really fun stuff with him. However, out of nowhere, you start to see subtle changes. It may be a loss of focus, or a lapse in concentration; it may be a cheeky recall, where you use that second cue, assuming your little darling just didn't hear you. Or it may be something more serious: your youngster may be the target of an unprovoked attack, or he may attack another dog without provocation.

So, your previously sweet, endearing pup has now turned into Cujo! And before you know it, his reputation has spread like wildfire with people drawing

When adolescence hits, you are left wondering what has happened to your perfect pup!

their dogs away as they see you approach, or picking up their children and shoving them into trees until you pass. Does any of this sound familiar?

Adolescence is a testing time to say the least, and this is when relationships are largely made or broken. Your young dog is transitioning from a puppy to an adult and, as a result, his body will be undergoing major changes. Hormones will be running amok, and the resulting behavioural changes are not because the dog is being 'bad' or 'naughty', it is because of physiological changes that he cannot control.

Male dogs emit testosterone from their system, which is like a belisha beacon signalling to other dogs that a young, adolescent male is present. Some dogs perceive this as a threat, and this can lead to 'unprovoked' acts of aggression, creating fear, defensive behaviour, and anxiety. Behaviour, deemed reactive, can often develop at this vulnerable time either because of a dog's direct experience, or from anxiety that develops following a traumatic event.

When female dogs enter adolescence, they will be due to season, which can cause unpredictable nervousness. This is where your previously happy-go-lucky baby starts to spook and act apprehensively without any due cause.

Adolescence can last up to approximately three years of age, depending on the breed and type of dog. The level of unpredictable behaviour will not be constant throughout this period; it will be more of a rollercoaster. You may get weeks, or months, where your dog's behaviour improves then, out of nowhere, you get a regression. To say it can be challenging and frustrating, would be an understatement.

For those who wish to train using positive reinforcement methods, the question is: how do I navigate this incredibly testing time, yet follow a path of reinforcement-based training?

Well, let's be clear from the outset. Remember Susan Garrett's mantra: "positive is not permissive". You may follow a reinforcement-based approach to training, but this doesn't mean you have to be a door mat. Dogs need clear boundaries and education, especially at this time.

Here are some simple points that should help you through your dog's adolescence:

High value reinforcement will get you through the difficult times.

1. You will need to become a master of management. The less your dog can rehearse inappropriate behaviour, the better. Anticipating a situation, and being prepared, is crucial. Employ the goodwill of others and set up learning experiences that you can control, and that mimic real life, rather then have unplanned, uncontrolled interactions.
2. Don't turn up to a gun fight armed with a knife... reinforcement is your friend! Ensure you control access to, and are always armed with, high value reinforcement. If you don't have the appropriate reinforcement for the situation, just avoid it.
3. Socialisation doesn't stop at puppyhood, it should continue throughout your dog's life. However, cherry-pick the dogs you allow your dog to interact with.

For example, avoid adolescent, entire males if you have an adolescent, entire male. At this age, due to hormonal changes, there is a higher chance of your dog being unpredictable and this could be a catalyst for an unnecessary altercation.

4. Don't prioritise your dog's 'proper' training at the most challenging times; his lack of concentration and limited focus will frustrate you and sour the association. Just stick to simple behaviours and focus on 'focus'. Prioritise your relationship.
5. One-on-one time is crucial, whether it be a five-minute training session, or a one-on-one walk. Take the time to relationship-build with your terrible teen. It is this relationship that will get you through the hard times.
6. Expect tantrums and tiaras. If your dog has an extreme reaction, stay calm, don't take it personally and, remember, reinforcement is key.
7. Your recall will probably disappear at some point during your dog's teenage phase. Increase your worth by feeding meals via training, and be mindful of pairing yourself with all things that are of value to your dog
8. Don't be afraid to scream, rant and vent – but not directly at the dog. That's what friends are for... Get it off your chest; it's ok to say your dog isn't your favourite 'person', just for the present.
9. Don't try to climb Mount Everest in one step. Pick your battles; some issues can wait for a more appropriate time, or they may not be so 'bad' that they warrant fixing. Your dog is still maturing, some things may just disappear with age. Be patient.
10. Accept that you will have good days and bad days – it's normal. This is not a permanent situation; you will get through it! Be patient, breathe, and go to your 'happy' place...

Finally, remember we have all been there. You will get through this; relationships are made of various phases, and this is just part of the journey. In years to come, you will chuckle at the testing antics and wonder what all the fuss was about!

Chapter Three

HOW TO BE AN EFFECTIVE CLICKER TRAINER

For me, there have been milestones in my career that have revolutionised my thinking beyond the realms of teaching dogs. Clicker training has been one of the most significant of these milestones.

I have always been a people watcher. I am fascinated by human behaviour and thinking, and try to work out what makes us do the things that we do, what drives us, what motivates us, and what affects our personality and the way we behave. When I was studying psychology at college, I became immersed in the concepts and thinking that underpin our actions, and – most importantly – how the concept of reinforcing behaviour and shaping applies to learning.

However, at that time, I was following a more traditional approach in relation to training dogs. I was applying the principles of learning theory, using reinforcement and breaking down behaviour, but I would still physically manipulate my dogs to show them what I wanted. This coincided with a shift in thinking – and a move towards clicker training which was taking place in the dog training community. Karen Pryor, who developed this method of training when working with dolphins, and Ian Dunbar, were becoming more widely recognised and increasingly respected by forward looking trainers.

Some years prior to my own personal dog training epiphany, I attended a seminar, given by Ian Dunbar, which looked at the use of food as positive reinforcement in training. But the seminar was focused on domestic training. I, like so many others, made the mistake of thinking that clicker training was fine for 'pet dogs' but not for 'real' training. I now laugh out loud at this short-sighted opinion.

It was only when a number of prominent obedience instructors started to use and advocate the use of a clicker that I started to sit up and take notice. I was intrigued, but I was torn between the desire to experiment with this new methodology, and scepticism regarding its value in the competition arena. How wrong can one person be...

MY TRAINING JOURNEY

I had several failed attempts at using a clicker in my own training, which I now know was due to my inability to understand the concepts. This all changed some 25 years ago when I was working with Scrunch, a feisty Chow cross, who started me on my journey towards positive reinforcement and shaping. Scrunch was not the easiest dog to train, and, surprisingly, my first light-bulb moment arose from something of a disaster. It all started when I was attending a training class and, among those in attendance, was a die-hard obedience competitor who was training her incredibly high drive Border Collie. At this time compulsion and punishment, in various forms and degrees, were widely accepted as the culture of how we trained dogs, both domestically and competitively.

On this particular occasion, the trainer was trying to deter her dog from pushing forward when she was doing heelwork. The dog was forging ahead of her, and she opted to 'fix' this by throwing a check chain in front of him. The hall had hard flooring and high ceilings, which meant that sounds reverberated like an orchestra playing at the Royal Albert Hall. At the sound of the check chain hitting the floor – and I can still replay this event as if it were yesterday – Scrunch was so terrified that she ran and hid under a chair.

She had been attending the hall for years yet, in a moment, she was so shocked she withdrew entirely. My attempts to entice her out, or comfort her, were futile. I was getting a lift home with a friend, and the event was so traumatic that Scrunch back-chained her fear so that, from then onwards, she was afraid to get into that vehicle on training nights. This went on for months. I tried everything, but there was nothing I could do to break this cycle of behaviour.

Then, one day, I had a light-bulb moment. Scrunch loved cheese, and I would often steal some of my Dad's favourite cheese when I was training her at home. This was at a time when using food was largely taboo, as it was considered a failing on the part of the handler. However, I felt I had nothing to lose. I had taught Scrunch countless tricks, all with cheese, and I knew she loved to do them. At the time, I didn't realise that it was my approach to training her that was the issue, not her ability to learn. In fact, I knew she was incredibly clever.

I started to use cheese as a reward, and, at the same time, I rattled a check chain in my hand. Scrunch didn't have an issue with the check chain itself, because she had been trained with one and wore a martingale collar. For several days, I paired the noise with food until she would hear the noise and visibly 'light up'. Looking back, I was 'counter conditioning' her association with the noise, and doing it in small increments.

Scrunch's aversion to going training had been ongoing for several months. She would often come training, but stay in the van. It was awful for us both. She hated it and so did I. Finally, I decided it was time to test the water, and take her into the hall. I deliberately picked an evening when the handler with the Border Collie, who had triggered the reaction, wasn't there.

Initially, Scrunch was tentative. But I was armed with my secret weapon. I fed her some cheese and within seconds she was back to the dog that I had taken training prior to the trauma. I say 'secret' because no one knew I was using this 'tool'. I daren't tell anyone about my crazy goings-on as the use of food was so frowned upon. Now, this story seems absurd but, at the time, this was the way things were.

I returned with Scrunch the following week and repeated the process. The next week, we had to contend with the handler and her Border Collie again. Faced with this situation now, I would be a lot more logical and systematic. But, in my naivety and ignorance, I stumbled on my first experience of using reinforcement to overcome behavioural issues, and the power of classical conditioning.

I explained that Scrunch had grown apprehensive about the thrown check chain and asked the handler if she would feed Scrunch with cheese before she brought her dog into the hall. Well that was it! It was an instant reaction – but this time in a positive way. All my layers of reinforcing had paid off, and Scrunch returned to the happy dog that she had always been. In fact, she started to drag me to the vehicle and squeal with excitement when we arrived at the hall. She overcame her fear to the extent that, not only was she happy around the 'offending' handler, she would also greet her like a long lost friend every time she saw her, and would be visibly excited if she got the chance to work alongside her. Incidentally, the handler stopped using the thrown chain method – so there was reinforcement for me, too!

The second example of the power of reinforcement was when I started to teach Scrunch to do flyball. Now this was a dog that didn't play, and had no ball drive. I had created some interest in toys, but not to the point where she would perceive them as reinforcement.

At this stage, I attended a week's course with Angela White, who was promoting the use of clickers to train behaviours and positive reinforcement as a means of resolving behavioural issues. During the week, we played around with various skills and games to teach us about clicker training.

I taught Scrunch to target a mat and catch a ball with a clicker, and then chained these two behaviours together so that she would target a mat and catch a ball for a click. This target was then placed on the flyball box and – *voila* – Scrunch would perform the behaviour. Again, my teaching was primitive and basic at best. I lumped behaviour and knew nothing about chaining or back chaining. However, what struck me was Scrunch's attitude to training. This was a dog that I had labelled as stubborn and indifferent to learning. She had no interest in anything I tried to teach her – with the exception of tricks – and now that I was putting this little series of behaviours in the category of tricks, Scrunch just loved it.

I completed this 'silly' little behaviour during the course of the week, and I would estimate that I spent no longer than 15 minutes working on it. Yet, with no further training and no rehearsals, Scrunch would perform this behaviour with the same level of enthusiasm and drive, years later. I rarely reinforced it, discarding it as a trick and therefore not worthy of reinforcement. I just assumed it was something Scrunch enjoyed doing. However, I was aware of the correlation between her attitude and how the behaviour was trained.

Since those early, unintentional interactions with clicker training, I went on to make several 'proper' attempts to use a clicker. And each time, I failed because my application was wrong. My resulting frustration caused me to persevere – and I am so glad that I did. Clicker training has revolutionised the way in which we teach and the way we train animals across the world. The concept of marking behaviour and 'capturing' it – communicating to the subject that their actions, decision making and thinking has a connection with reinforcement – has allowed an octopus to take a picture and a dog to fly a plane! Its power and potency cannot be under-estimated.

GETTING STARTED

I personally prefer to use a box clicker, as it is louder and more 'definite' in its sound. However, if you have a more noise sensitive dog you may wish to use a button clicker. The same effect can also be achieved by using a distinct 'clicker' word.

For me, the click acts like a behaviour camera. It captures the exact behaviour or, eventually, behaviours that the dog is performing when he hears the click. Often a clicker is misused, and its power is watered down by inappropriate use or mistiming. Animal trainer Bob Bailey says that a marker is a precision tool and, just as a surgeon would use a scalpel, a trainer should use a clicker.

To charge up a word, or a clicker, to have value is a simple process, and should not take more than one training session:

- Find a relatively sterile environment to work in. I tend to use food when I first charge up a clicker as it's easy to do several repetitions. So, make sure you have sufficient food, and choose something your dog considers to be high value.
- Press your clicker, and deliver the food within one second. If your dog is noise sensitive, you can opt to use a word. For dogs with impaired hearing, you can pair a flashlight with food, and this can act as your clicker.
- When choosing a word to use as your 'click', try not to use a word that you are likely to use in everyday communication, and thus de-sensitise your dog to the power of the word. Personally, I don't like 'yes' or 'good' as I use them too readily. My clicker words are 'win' and 'yip'.

TOP TIP
You can undo or change your clicker word at any time by stopping pairing reinforcement with the click/word.

- Test that your dog understands the click or clicker word. If the dog turns back to you for food, it is clear that he understands that a click/clicker word means a reward will follow. When you see this behaviour, you are ready to start to clicker training.
- Inevitably, there will be times when you get your timing wrong and mis-click. In this situation, I always deliver a reward – even if I am not marking the behaviour I want. I do not want to risk souring my dog's association with the clicker. As far as he is concerned, a click always means he will get a reward.

Clicker training, like all methods, is only as effective as its operator.

SHAPING AND LURING

There are numerous ways to teach a new behaviour, and having a clear idea of what you want will help you decide how to approach it. Basically, there are two methods of reinforcement training: shaping and luring. Both methods have their advocates – and I, personally, believe both have a valid place in dog training. However, knowing which to do, and when, is not quite so easy!

Shaping is the term used when we reward incremental steps in a dog's offered behaviour as he progresses towards our goal position or action. Luring is where you guide the dog into position using food or a toy.

The pros and cons of shaping and luring can be explained with the following analogy:

Imagine that you come to my house, and I suggest you attend one of my classes as a guest. You decide to drive your own vehicle and follow me to the venue. We do this several times until, on one particular day, I am unable to attend and I suggest that you go without me. How confident would you be to find your way? Perhaps? Maybe?

On previous journeys, where was your focus and concentration? Most likely, your attention was fixed on keeping my vehicle in sight.

Now think of the contrast. Instead of allowing you to follow my car, I give you directions to get to the venue…."go to the end of the road, turn right…. go to the large roundabout with the garage on it, straight over that and head past the Red Lion pub…" and so on.

Initially, you may have an issue finding your way to the venue. You may even get lost, and find an alternative route. Eventually you would find your way there. Over time, you would be able to get there more quickly and with more efficiency.

Now, imagine if there was a roadblock on your regular route. The chances are that you could still find your way due to your in-depth knowledge of the area. On your previous journeys where you were 'lost', you were actually learning about the area and, as a result, you could find an alternative route with little effort.

This is the difference between shaping and luring.

Shaping: The dog works out what is being reinforced as he progresses towards the desired goal.

Luring: The handler shows the dog what to do by luring with a treat.

43

The Modern Principles of Shaping

By Karen Pryor

1. Be prepared before you start. Be ready to click/treat immediately when the training session begins. When shaping a new behaviour, be ready to capture the very first tiny inclination the animal gives you toward your goal behaviour. This is especially true when working with a prop such as a target stick or a mat on the ground.

2. Ensure success at each step. Break behaviour down into small enough pieces that the learner always has a realistic chance to earn a reinforcer.

3. Train one criterion at a time. Shaping for two criteria or aspects of a behaviour simultaneously can be very confusing. One click should not mean two different criteria.

4. Relax criteria when something changes. When introducing a new criterion or aspect of the skill, temporarily relax the old criteria for previously mastered skills.

5. If one door closes, find another. If a particular shaping procedure is not progressing, try another way.

6. Keep training sessions continuous. The animal should be continuously engaged in the learning process throughout the session. He should be working the entire time, except for the moment he's consuming/enjoying his reinforcer. This also means keeping a high rate of reinforcement.

7. Go back to kindergarten, if necessary. If a behaviour deteriorates, quickly revisit the last successful approximation or two so that the animal can easily earn reinforcers.

8. Keep your attention on your learner. Interrupting a training session gratuitously by taking a phone call, chatting, or doing something else that can wait often cause learners to lose momentum and get frustrated by the lack of information. If you need to take a break, give the animal a "goodbye present," such as a small handful of treats.

9. Stay ahead of your learner. Be prepared to "skip ahead" in your shaping plan if your learner makes a sudden leap.

10. Quit while you're ahead. End each session with something the learner finds reinforcing. If possible, end a session with a strong behavioural response, but, at any rate, try to end with your learner still eager to go on.

Be patient when you are teaching a new behaviour and only shape one criterion at a time.

CLICKER POSITIVES

Some of the key positives I have discovered include the following:

- A clicker allows me to mark random behaviour and reward, thus increasing the chances of it occurring again. I can also shape individual traits into my dog's work to strengthen the behaviour I want.

  For example, my young Collie, Scooter, is a real softie and, although he is very willing, when I first got him he would prefer a cuddle, or to curl up on the sofa, rather than playing tug or engaging in a way that was useful or productive. I applied the rules of clicker training and built and shaped any resemblance of drive and power he had. Over time this became strong enough to use in his training. Any flicker of what I wanted was rewarded; this, in turn, developed and grew stronger.

- I can reward the dog for each part of an exercise as opposed to waiting for the exercise to be completed. By rewarding the parts, I can make the overall exercise stronger. For example, if my dog does a particularly brilliant pick-up on retrieve, I can isolate this part of the exercise and reinforce this component, thus increasing the chances of the brilliant pick up happening again.
- I can alter an exercise by increasing the reward for the parts I like, and not rewarding the parts I dislike. For example, in the case of a dog that has learnt to be over the top, I would reward for the minutest sign of calm behaviour, making the dog try less to get more.
- The clicker allows me to gain a lot more for far less. The dog learns to push me in order to get his reward. I can use shaping – allowing the dog to 'offer' behaviours – to build any type of behaviour I want, from standing on a balance cushion to precision heelwork. The method is only as good as your imagination. I don't have to run round like a headless chicken to get the dog working for me once the idea of how to get rewarded is set in his mind.
- I have found that when using a clicker I can put duration on exercises fairly quickly. This ultimately improves concentration and stamina. However, if this is not done systematically and logically, it can induce stress and create a grey area for the dog (see Signs Of Stress, Page 48). This is ok; learning in itself can be stressful. Just reward any improvement and, in time, your dog will see any failure as a chance to show you how fantastic he is and try even harder to get it right.

CLICKER PITFALLS
There are some areas where clicker training can work against you – but, more often than not, the fault lies with the handler rather than the method:
- The clicker can encourage laziness on the handler's part. The clicker is not a magic tool that produces a dog that loves to learn. It still requires

hard work from the handler. The danger is that the handler becomes too reliant on the clicker, and is unable to function without it. There is also a risk that the handler fails to put 'himself' into the training, and relies on the food or toy to communicate the information. For me, training is an extension of my relationship with my dog. It is an expression of the dog's perception of me, and I want my dog to want to be around me and to engage with me. This has to be a two-way street.

- The clicker can create a false illusion; the dog appears to understand an exercise completely but, in fact, it needs to be generalised and proofed before learning is established. This can occur with any method but seems to happen more frequently with clicker training. It has been found that information that the learner acquires for himself – rather then information where he is 'shown' – is far more powerful. But this information needs to be taken to lots of environments to create a strong understanding.
- The clicker methodology is based on scientific research carried out by people who were not necessarily involved with dogs in a domestic situation. It can therefore appear to lack emotional nuances and passion, and create a dog that lacks personality. You can't create personality without letting yourself get involved! A sound understanding of the theory is imperative, but there are idiosyncrasies that books and DVDs will never cover. You must be prepared to listen to your gut and your heart.
- A lot of clicker training is based on mental manipulation. This can be challenging, and produce anxiety in the dog. As a handler you may not be inflicting physical discomfort, but you could be putting him under mental pressure.
- The clicker is always clear about what is being rewarded, but this can make it difficult to isolate behaviours. For example, you have taught a foot target and you are now working on head position. The dog adjusts his head position and foot at the same time, and you click. From the dog's perspective, it is unclear which behaviour you are rewarding.
- You get what you click. If you train your dog and reward every 30 seconds you will get a dog that is only capable of doing 30 seconds' of work. This is a classic error made by clicker trainers in competitive dog sports. Susan Garrett, pioneer of *Say Yes Dog Training* and author of *Shaping Success* and *Ruff*

Signs of Stress

When you are training, observe your dog closely for signs of stress or anxiety. This may include:
- licking lips
- vocalisation
- avoidance
- averting eye contact
- sniffing the ground
- air sniffing
- panting
- overall demeanour

Each of these, on their own, may not be a cause of concern. However, in the context of shaping and training, an accumulation of these behaviours should be taken as a sign that the dog is stressed, so you will need to review your training method.

Turning away and avoiding eye contact is a sure sign of stress.

Love, refers to this as the D.A.S.H. principle. To be an effective clicker trainer, you need the four components –Desire, Accuracy, Speed and Habitat – when teaching any behaviour.

THE BIG FOUR (AS IDENTIFIED BY BOB BAILEY)

Training success depends on four crucial factors:
1. Timing
2. Rate of reinforcement
3. Criteria
4. Consistency

1. **Timing:** This is fundamental to any type of training, regardless of the discipline, method or animal. It would be wonderful if we could rely on a God given gift which allowed us to read and react to any given situation – but, unfortunately, it doesn't always happen this way. Even if you have excellent timing and the ability to read a dog, working to improve these skills will help you in the long run and make you a far better trainer

2. **Rate of reinforcement:** How often you reward a behaviour is critical to learning. You need to ensure that you are reinforcing the behaviour at the appropriate interval for the dog. This is dependent on the dog's experience, understanding, environment and value of reinforcement. Reinforcing frequently is key in the learning stages but reinforcing too often, when your dog is experienced and competent in executing a behaviour, can lead to poor performance. The appropriate rate of reinforcement is critical for the outcome.
   - A constant rate of reinforcement is where the dog is reinforced every time he performs a behaviour.
   - A fixed rate of reinforcement is where the reinforcement is predictable and fixed.
   - A variable schedule of reinforcement is where the delivery of reinforcement is unpredictable and varied.

3. **Criteria:** The standard or guidance for which reinforcement is going to be given. For example, when I say, "down", my dog adopts a sphinx down in one fluid motion with this elbows on the ground. Any other approximation of the behaviour – a sloppy position, or a delay before getting into position – will not be reinforced.

49

4. **Consistency:** Adopting clear criteria will ensure that you are consistent in what you reinforce, and this helps your dog to understand what you want. Pre-planning your sessions, or just having a clear goal, will make your training more effective and efficient.

This will ensure that you are consistent in what you are training and therefore reinforcing.

KEY TO EFFECTIVE CLICKER TRAINING

- To improve timing, ask a friend to bounce a ball and click when the ball makes contact with the ground. This will help improve your ability to judge something visually and anticipate the ball touching the ground.
- Choose a word and click every time you hear it on the TV during a programme. For example, you could click every time you hear "Rickkkkky" on *Eastenders* – although, be warned, you may get RSI (repetitive strain injury)!
- If you have the opportunity, handle dogs of different breeds and abilities. This will help you develop a 'feel' for what you like and don't like, and allow you to form a visual reference in your mind of what it is you want from your own dog. This will inevitably improve your timing, as you will be able to aim more clearly for what you want.
- Try to pre-empt the error before it occurs, or be ready for the likelihood that it will occur. This may seem obvious, but you would be surprised how many times handlers allow their dogs to make the same mistake in the vain hope that they will "be ready next time". For example, if your dog has anticipated the retrieve three times on the trot, there is a high chance he will do the same on the fourth. You need to do something to counteract this.
- Be prepared to make mistakes – we all do! Accept this is part and parcel of learning. Consider it feedback and try not to make the same mistake twice.

These are just a few simple ideas to get you thinking, experiment and develop your own ideas. This is called dog training – everything is based on trial and error!

My Rules of Clicker Training

Clicker training is a way of life for me and I have my own take on the most effective way of using it. This is what I have learnt:

1. While having a dog understanding a mechanical clicker is a fundamental of clicker training, it is far more advantageous to have a dog that understands a verbal 'click' word, which has the same relevance.

2. Using reward specific markers (see page 61) to tell your dog what he is receiving, and from where, can avoid confusion, and prevent anxiety, over-arousal, loss of speed and ambiguous moments in your training.

3. While clicker training should be clear, involving minimal interference as the dog works out what you want, this does not mean you have to be an impartial observer. Your relationship with your dog, encouraging him and boosting his confidence, is the most important factor in this process. Communicate your joy and gratification – don't cheerlead but celebrate with your dog!

4. The power of the clicker is often watered down as people have a tendency to use it randomly, almost frivolously. I refrain from using my actual 'click' until the dog does exactly what I want him to do. This does not mean I can't reinforce. I just withhold the click until the dog 'nails' it. This clarifies and consolidates exactly what I want him to do.

5. Allowing your dog the space to think is a good thing! Furrowing his brow and using his grey matter will ultimately create clarity and confidence. Let him think!

6. Shaping and clicker training creates a feel-good factor for both dog, and handler. This is far more potent then any treat! It is literally addictive, so use it to your advantage.

7. While it is imperative to consider what you click, it is just as important to think about how you reinforce. What, when, why, how and where – the five elements of reinforcement are crucial. You can click a brilliant sit stay, but if you keep reinforcing out of position, you will create instability. You get what you click, but you also get what you reinforce, so ensure you are reinforcing what you want.

8. Be sure to check that you and your dog are on the same page, as what you click isn't necessarily what you want. Changing the picture, the approach, your position or even the context will help you assess if you

and your dog are in sync. You can invest a lot of clicks into the wrong behaviour if you're not careful.

9. While there is great joy in clicking single behaviours, for sports dogs you need to evolve this to behaviour chains (see Chapter Ten) and have your behaviour on a variable schedule of reinforcement. Without this piece of the puzzle, you will be under-preparing your dog for competition.

10. Remember to 'train hard and fight easy'. Over train and ask for more in training so what you ask for in competition is considerably easier.

11. If you make a mistake, don't be afraid to go back, but don't feel obliged to 'click' this. You can do what I call 'fast tracking'. This is where I take the dog through all the stages of what I am training, but in a relatively short period of time. I can do this for one reinforcement or for a fuss. Then try a harder version of the behaviour, but not necessarily the piece you are struggling with, and then click this. If you continually take a dog back to kindergarten you can create learned helplessness (see page 57) and the dog learns to quit, or wait for you to help him, which is not needed.

12. Training doesn't always have to end on a good repetition (see page 113). Reinforcement-based training is about information rather than judgment. So ending on a mistake or an error is information. Sometimes it's better to stop and abort training rather then soldier on.

13. Training shouldn't be about drilling and toiling over extended periods of time. Little and often works best. You can build duration as a separate entity but, while teaching, short and sweet works best.

14. Thinking laterally about what your dog considers to be reinforcement is crucial. Swimming, chasing birds, the hosepipe, getting in my vehicle, sprinting off with other dogs, are just some of the reinforcers I have used with my own dogs. Harnessing their power will create a dog that sees you as the best person in the world. As you have access to Disney World, they just have to have the right entrance ticket!

15. Teach first before adding arousal or excitement. These are both going to challenge the dog, so ensure he knows what you want first. Arousal should be like the volume on your iPod: be in control, so you can turn it up and turn it down.

Chapter Four

DOES CLICKER TRAINING WORK FOR EVERY DOG?

C licker training has transformed the way I work with dogs, increasing my effectiveness in communicating with them, and enhancing my relationship with them. But does clicker training work for every dog? My findings are based purely on my experience as a dog trainer and teacher, going back some 25 years. I have no scientific proof to support what I have written; my conclusions are purely based on observation, working with students, and working with my own dogs.

HOW REINFORCEMENT WORKS

Every dog is operant, which means that every dog can work out very quickly how his behaviour triggers or elicits reinforcement. So the dog that raids the dustbin will soon work out that it is filled with 'treasures', or the dog that runs off when called, may find out that rabbits spontaneously pop up.

But there are degrees of 'operancy', i.e. some dogs are better at problem solving and working out these patterns than others. This is no different to you or me; we all are better or worse at certain things. Some people are great at maths, others English…it's the same with dogs – they all have varying degrees of ability to learn.

With clicker training and shaping, we are largely interested in how quickly

Clicker training works wonders in most circumstances and for most dogs – but not all...

the dog cottons on to the game we are playing. Can he solve the simple equation in order to earn the reward we have on offer? This is essentially what shaping and clicker training is all about – a series of problems the dog has to solve in order to receive his reinforcement.

Every dog can do it – but are all dogs best suited to clicker training? In short, I believe the simple answer is no, not all dogs suit clicker training. Shock, horror! I can hear you gasp as you read this. What if you have a dog that isn't suited to clicker training and shaping? How can you tell, and what should you do?

Ok, let's take a deep breath and review this statement. No, not all dogs are suited to being trained using purely shaping behaviour, due largely to type, genetic predisposition and character.

I have used a clicker in my training for about 15 years, and I have been a pure clicker trainer for about 11 years. My evolution has been from traditional training to clicker training, so from a 'let me show you what I want' trainer, to a 'you work it out' trainer. One of my first experiences of clicker training was with a red and white Border Collie, called Springa, who was from strong British obedience lines. I always said he wasn't the brightest of dogs, but now I look back and attribute this largely to methodology.

Springa was born in 2000, and was the first dog that I attempted to clicker train. However I was still a 'show and tell' trainer, and I wanted to combine this with the 'you work it out' method. I had made a conscious decision to combine the two, as I wasn't totally sold on clicker training and still had one foot in the

54

traditional camp. I started clicker training Springa as a pup and, to be honest, I didn't note any significant advantages with what he learnt and how he learnt. I was still doing a combination of 'traditional' stuff in the midst of my 'clickering'!

I persisted for a while, and quickly deduced that clicker training didn't work, and had little benefit for that dog as he wasn't bright enough to get it. I retired my clicker to my training bag and carried on my merry way. Occasionally, I would use a clicker to mark behaviour, or I would use a clicker word, normally 'yes' or 'good' – and it seemed to be reasonably effective – but not to the point where I was prepared to commit.

However, I made a few distinct observations with regard to Springa, and I later realised that these would be crucial to my eventual immersion into clicker training.

Springa hated silences – where he had to work things out – and so did I. When he was learning, and I was waiting to see what he would offer, Springa would often get visibly stressed or show displacement behaviour. He hadn't been exposed to any correction and yet he would still show signs of being uncomfortable. In these instances, I would show him what I wanted and he would instantly cotton on, and so we could move forward. In competitions, when I was under pressure, Springa would display this same pattern of behaviour.

At the same time as I was training Springa, I used a clicker and re-trained my competition dog, Tai. Although very closely related to Springa, Tai was a totally different type of dog. He had a microchip brain, and was naturally biddable and smart. So I knew that clicker training did work – you just needed the right dog. Or did you?

Springa and Tai were the catalyst for a new way of thinking, allowing me to open up a totally different path in my dog training. For this I am forever grateful.

Here are the lessons that they taught me, and I am sure they will resonate with your own experiences of teaching and shaping:

- Crossover dogs can often take longer to 'get' shaping as they have learnt to wait for 'help'. Be patient, and click the dog for smaller behaviours.
- There are types of dogs that struggle with offering behaviour as they are almost predisposed to wait to be shown. With these types of dogs, shaping is a huge asset in getting the best from them. It is worth struggling through the process, as it will serve you well in the long run.

- Any dog can work things out. It's handlers who struggle with awkward silences.
- There are two simple rules of shaping: firstly, make it easy enough for the dog to be successful; secondly, provide sufficient reward.
- Luring can be a short-term solution to a long-term issue. You need to use it wisely and strategically, otherwise it can lead to learned helplessness (see page 57).

RESISTANCE TO SHAPING

The next dog that I trained was a Malinois male, called Strut. Every dog you train will teach you lessons and Strut, my first Malinois, was a steep learning curve. He was from working lines and was my first dog of that strength, power and type.

By this stage I was prepared to admit that clicker training had some benefits, so I decided to have another go with Strut.

Strut was not a genius, but he was not dim either. He had great food drive, play drive and was biddable. To begin with, I attempted to free shape behaviour – waiting for him to initiate a behaviour. What a total disaster that turned out to be! Strut hated shaping – he just didn't 'get it'. He would displace, go to leave training or clam up.

I then started work on a duration hand touch. I had taught numerous dogs to do this relatively simple behaviour, but with Strut it was a major struggle. For a month, I kept on trying. He would get to multiple hand touches, and no more. As this was a crucial skill for his training, it caused a lot of frustration for both of us. Strut would again display the same pattern of displacement as when he was being free shaped. He would clam up, displace and disengage. There was no problem with anything else he was learning; he was grasping concepts quickly and making great progress. I just couldn't get the duration hand touch.

By now, I was starting to question whether I should abort the hand touch training and try something else. One day, out of pure frustration, I decided to try a different tactic. Our training session started with some nice, easy stuff – and he was brilliant. So I decided to try the dreaded hand touch again. Rather then see if Strut would bring his nose to my hand, I put my hand on his nose. I held it it there for five seconds and then clicked. I repeated this a second time.

The third time, as I moved my hand toward Strut, he intercepted its approach and adopted the perfect hand touch position! He stayed there until I clicked.

I then held my hand and waited. As if having an 'aha' moment, he confidently shoved his nose into my palm and remained there wagging his tail. I clicked and ended our session. Clear as the nose on my face, I knew Strut had got it. Within a week, he went from struggling to offer a two second hand touch in a static position, to doing a constant hand touch on the move.

LEARNED HELPLESSNESS

So it appeared that I had gained from showing Strut what I wanted him to do. He was not a dog that wanted to think for himself, and this was a trait he showed throughout his career. I therefore opted to show him what I wanted rather then shape him.

I saw this trait with other Malinois. They struggled to think for themselves, and were quick to reach a point of frustration. I also saw it in working gundogs, strong working line Border Collies and other dogs that were purpose bred to do a job.

This got me thinking about the type of dogs that showed this same trait. They all fit the same description. They were:

• Biddable
• Tenacious
• Bred from working lines
• Didn't want to think for themselves

Thinking about these qualities, I realised that the ability to think for themselves had almost been bred out of them. Most of the dogs displaying this trait were either from lines, or of a type, that did well with traditional training. They loved to work and to be shown what to do.

This was the prevalent approach to their training, and therefore the dogs that were most receptive to this approach would be most successful and therefore included in the genetic mix. They would be the dogs most likely to be bred from, as they best fitted the mould. There would be minimal scope for free thinking or lateral thinking. This wouldn't have been perceived as an asset. I could see this in Strut – he fitted this description to a tee.

The short term gain of having a dog, such as Strut, who lacked the ability to think for himself was that I could teach him something relatively quickly and with little fuss. I simply showed him what I wanted and he would repeat the behaviour. Easy, right? In the short-term, yes. However in the long term, in pressurised situations – for example if he made an error or I did – he would need me to bail him out. He developed learned helplessness: "If I make a mistake, I don't do anything as Dad will come to the rescue." This created a bigger issue when in competition as Strut wouldn't recover from a mistake, and he also struggled greatly with a change of pattern. He couldn't problem solve.

Now, this is something that I would work to overcome by teaching the dog to offer behaviours which develop the ability think for himself. I use shaping, and challenge the dog via shaping, to think even when he gets frustrated, displaced or wants to shut down.

I have now used this approach with numerous dogs – my own, those I have taught, and those attending seminars and workshops – and it has resulted in dogs that can think while in a state of high arousal, are unlikely to shut down and are willing to keep on trying. I can teach the dogs to think laterally and problem solve. I can also build their confidence to work through struggles.

CONCEPT TRAINING

This approach to clicker training teaches your dog concepts of learning prior to actually starting the 'formal' process of teaching an exercise.

The following are some of the concepts that will help prepare your dog to learn new behaviours and skills:

- Lateral thinking.
- Resilience to failure.
- A positive emotional condition response to 'punishment' or no reinforcement (see Chapter Seven).
- Coping with any stress and frustration that learning can impose, and life may present (see Chapter Eight).
- Clear understanding of a release cue.
- Clear understanding of a 'click'.
- Switching between toys and food (see Chapter Nine).
- Channeling drive, and states of arousal (see Chapter Eleven).
- Placement of reinforcement specific markers (see page 59).
- Understanding of your dog's specific learning pattern.

There are many more concepts that can be taught and 'explained' to your dog prior to teaching a specific skill that may be of importance to you.

REWARD SPECIFIC MARKERS

As I have evolved as a trainer, I have expanded my toolbox to include more skills that have enhanced my dogs' understanding and created clarity. Placement of reinforcement specific markers has had a massive effect on my dogs'ability to learn.

I had known about reward-specific markers and, like everything in dog training that is 'new', I tended to be cynical and questioned its value – blame the policing instinct! However, it was a dog that forced me to reconsider. Several years ago, my student and friend had a phenomenal Giant Schnauzer called Fingal, who was the first of his breed to be trained to IPO 3, to represent his country at the World Championships and was trained with positive reinforcement.

However, Fingal had a constant struggle with heelwork when he was in a heightened state of arousal. He would start to push his position, and although he would not go forward, his back end would start to flare out. We battled this issue with varying degrees of success, but nothing seemed to click.

I had known of the concept of reward specific markers but hadn't totally embraced it. However it was Shade Whitesel, fellow Fenzi Dog Sports Academy faculty member, who really got me thinking about how to use them.

We set about teaching Fingal a reward specific marker that told him to turn away in an anti-clockwise circle when he was in the correct heelwork position, and then get the reinforcement from behind. Previously we had trained to click his adjustments, but because of his emotional conditioned response to the 'click' and its generic meaning, plus his lightning fast reactions, we often failed to position the reinforcement appropriately.

When he understood that the reinforcement was coming in a specific place, and in a specific manner, he instantly had an 'aha' moment. Within minutes, his behaviour changed and what he had been rehearsing for some time, instantly improved. We extended this to his bite work, and toy interaction which, again, created clarity for him in how, when and where he was to bite.

Shaping a Behaviour

I start with a simple behaviour, such as 'get in/on a box'. I set the dog up to be successful by making the box appropriately sized and constructed so the dog can easily step into or on to it.

In contrast to other trainers I don't use a clicker, either verbally or mechanically, to mark behaviour in the initial stages. The reason for this is that, often, the attempts or offered responses are nothing like the end behaviour I am looking for.

I want the click to capture a precise and exact behaviour, and also establish a distinct means of communication. If my dog is sniffing the box, and my end goal is for him to step into it, I wouldn't use a clicker to mark the sniff. I could praise, acknowledge and reinforce the behaviour but, for my dogs, a click says: "Bingo! You've got it". This approach to clicker training creates an incredibly clicker savvy dog who can learn in seconds, and will identify the exact behaviour I have clicked instantly. This creates clarity for the dog.

Reinforcing a behaviour doesn't have to be dependent on a click. So I can praise and reinforce all the efforts, but save my click for the exact behaviour I am aiming for. When I start this process, I would also jackpot the dog – giving a bonus reward – after the click to further enhance its power.

When the dog is confidently performing the desired behaviour, I reduce the size of the box. This presents a physical challenge to the dog, and can create frustration and a level of anxiety. By working through this process, I teach the dog to cope with both. He is also learning to think and process information while in this heightened state of arousal. This is a crucial skill for dogs to develop.

By taking this approach to shaping, I have the means of creating a dog that has several key traits:

- He truly understands what the click means – "you nailed it! You did exactly what I wanted".
- He quickly continues to offer the clicked behaviour and stops offering

the variations. This creates a dog that is confident in what he is doing so there are fewer repetitions or wasted attempts.

- He is learning a 'language' which is systematically taught, and therefore opens up a channel of communication that is both clear and salient to him.

- He can think while in a high state of arousal, and can work through frustration.

- He can cope with stress and frustration away from sports training, for example, in general life. This is a key skill for dogs that have a tendency to be reactive, as you have the means of teaching an appropriate response when they get frustrated or stressed.

A clicker savvy dog is very quick to learn new behaviours.

Since Fingal's lesson, I have used this approach more and more...creating clarity for my dogs and as an antidote for any confusion that generic click words can create.

So let me clarify a question that I posed earlier. 'Are all dogs suited to clicker training?'

No..., not if they have had a history of conflicting information, or a trainer that fails to break down behaviours into achievable chunks and does not communicate the information clearly.

This is empowering as it means the responsibility falls on our shoulders to clarify what we want our dogs to learn in a way that makes sense them.

This means being unafraid to throw away the rulebook, move away from the well-worn path that is tradition, and step outside the box.

Be the trainer your dog wants, needs and deserves.

All things become possible if you follow the path of positive reinforcement.

Chapter Five

BUILDING PLAY

P lay is a vital component in the way I train. As far as the dog is concerned, work should equal play, and play should equal work. The two should be seamless.

The advantage of play is that I, as the handler, get some sort of reward from it. With food, the dog eats it and I get little satisfaction from the process.

Play is great for relationship building and stress relief. A good game can break the tension if you reach a sticky point in training, and can therefore help to progress a session.

My aim is for the dog to engage happily in a tug session, do a play retrieve, chase a moving toy and a still toy – and I want this on any toy I produce.

Don't fool yourself, play is all about igniting your dog's predatory instincts.

Photo: Juliet Dearbergh.

A VOYAGE OF DISCOVERY

Knowing what motivates your dog is the key question. It is the biggest and most important question you can ask, and it needs to be asked constantly throughout your dog's life, taking into account specific environments, situations and different distractions.

Your dog's DNA – his genetic make-up – often gives clues as to how best to approach and introduce play. For example, many of the gundogs naturally want to retrieve, terrier types want to hang on to a toy and worry it, and herding breeds are attracted by movement. If you have scant knowledge of your dog's genetic background, observation will be crucial. Whenever I get a 'new' dog (this may be a puppy, a rescued/rehomed dog, or a dog that has come to me for training), my first task is to fathom out what motivates him. I gain this powerful and vital information by observing the dog and finding out what he wants

Ideally this would be toys and food – but this is not always the case. What constitutes reinforcement for a dog is determined by him, and him alone; finding out exactly what this is can be the most challenging part.

UNDERSTANDING PLAY

What does 'play' mean to your dog? Whether we wish to acknowledge it or not, dogs are predators and the process of play is replicating hunting, pursuing, chasing, capturing and killing prey. The behavioural traits we see a dog exhibit in play are exactly the same traits we see when dogs hunt. Chasing, grabbing, tugging and shaking are all acts of capturing prey. In order to create 'play', we must first accept this link and then work out how prey is likely to act, look and behave.

When I am first working with a puppy or an adult dog, I will have an inclination as to how to interact with him, and how to introduce play, based on his genetic heritage. So for example, with a Border Collie that likes things that move fast, I present the toy in a way that incites chase, whilst a gundog may want to carry the toy and hold on to it while you interact with him.

Each dog is different – even within breeds and breed types – so be prepared to adapt. If your dog is sensitive and is over-faced by play, take your time and don't rush the process. All dogs will play, but whether they perceive this as reinforcement is another thing altogether.

Some dogs, like people, have preferences. My German Spitz, Sonic, is a great example of a dog that most definitely prefers food. He plays and is happy to do so, but if I offered him a piece of steak or a tug toy, I know exactly what the answer would be: "medium rare, please Dad!" However, the key is to create desire and value in as many different types of reinforcement as you possibly can, whether it be toys, food, physical interaction, games, sounds, or environmental reinforcements.

When I start training, I use the dog's allocated meals as training treats throughout the day. With puppies this is easy as they are fed several times a day, so it's a natural process to use their food to train them. But I adopt the same procedure with an older dog. The reason for this is that I want to create focus for me. Mealtimes are likely to be the highlight of a dog's day, so harnessing this 'reward' is a key way to create a dog that values you and your interaction.

My aim is to build a relationship with my dogs where they want to be around me, where they trust me and value me. This starts with pairing the things they want with me. So, being aware of what your dog finds reinforcing is crucial to creating that relationship.

ASSESSING YOUR DOG FOR TUG

Teaching your dog to tug sounds simple, but it is one of the most common areas where people encounter issues with their dogs – and the reason for this is polar opposites. It is either because the dog won't tug or because the dog is so keen he loses control of the game. So understanding the importance of teaching a tug is massively important.

When I first introduce toys to a dog, I equate this to starting a conversation with someone with whom I want I to make a long lasting impression. This could be a first date, a meeting with the bank manager, or a job interview. Think of a situation that requires you to be aware of your actions, body language and words. If I wade in with my size 12 feet – without thinking about what I am doing – I could cause serious offence. However, if I don't create a great first impression, the chances are I won't get a second meeting!

Being too intrusive versus being unnoticeable. This is a hard line to tread.

If you go in too strongly, you could be off-putting for life, but going in too passively will make you a non-event. What you need to do is to make an impression that allows you to work out your next move. This is exactly the same when you are starting play.

Working out how to present the tug-toy to your dog is crucial for building tug drive, and for establishing an interactive relationship.

In the initial assessment phase, my aim is to gauge the dog's natural drive and find out what floats his boat. I pick a location that is quiet. Ideally, there should be no distractions but if there are any, they must be low level. I start by allowing the dog to relax and check out his environment. I don't want to ask him to engage with a toy when he is investigating his surroundings.

I then start to interact with the dog – without even bringing a toy into the equation. I like to sit on the floor so I can work at the dog's level. If you can't sit on the floor, sit on a chair. If you have a larger dog, standing may be more appropriate, but be mindful that this can be off putting for some dogs.

I initially fuss the dog and allow him to interact with me in a quiet manner.

I then momentarily stop the interaction. This is a brief 'silence' which then allows me to send the dog an invitation to play. When I am ready,

The toy should mimic the movement of a live animal to incite the dog's interest.
Photo: Juliet Dearbergh.

I casually produce a toy. I start with a chaser toy and move it along the floor to see if he shows any chase instinct. I use a toy that allows me to create movement – something that is brightly coloured and of a material or texture that is like fur or hair. Again, this is to replicate 'prey'.

I start with some low-key interaction, but not necessarily getting the dog too excited or aroused. This is because I want to work out the dog's reaction to the toy, rather than upping his arousal and creating drive for the toy. These are two very different things. I want to assess and understand if the dog has value for toys without any hyping up from me. I want to determine if he values toys naturally or whether I have to create a desire for them.

After presenting the toy and creating a little movement, I make it disappear from sight, hiding it behind my back. I keep the movement moderate at this stage, which allows me to increase it if I don't get a reaction.

I am looking to see if the dog shows any interest in the toy. I equate this to to a dog wandering in a field and then a rabbit suddenly sticks its head out from a hole. Does he notice, or does he carry on sniffing? So depending on the reaction, I decide on the next step. If the dog ignores the toy, I may try again and increase the movement, or leave the toy in sight for longer. When you do this, think of how prey moves in relation to the predator. There will be a story that unfolds as the prey attempts to elude the grasp of its pursuer.

Movement of the toy should always be erratic. The prey won't move in perfect linear motion. This is a classic mistake that is often made when a handler presents a tug-toy in a dead straight line, and moves it too fast or too slowly for the dog. Moving the toy in curves, zig-zags and arches is far more realistic, and keeping the motion at a medium tempo – at least to start with – is a safe bet. You are looking for your dog to show interest in the toy. This interest may be minimal, it may be super intense. It doesn't matter, but you will need to tread carefully when planning your next move.

If the dog shows any interest, I allow him to approach the toy and I create movement away from him. This is to incite chase.

If he pursues the toy, I allow him to capture it, and I have a brief game of tug. The dog's reaction dictates if I end the session at this point or continue. The most I would do is allow the dog a very brief tug, which he would win.

I would repeat this a few times, and end the session there. The actual play should last for seconds, if that. When I end the session, I don't implement any control. I merely remove the toy and leave the dog wanting more.

If the dog fails to show any interest, I would try a different type of toy and create movement and sound to try to get the dog's attention. This might be a hessian bite bar which I could thump on the ground; I might bounce a ball so it makes erratic movements; I might offer a plastic bottle, a rolled up newspaper, or a toy with food secreted inside – anything that might get a response.

In my experience, there are a lot of dogs that don't show much, if any, interest in the toy at first – especially those that have a previous bad history of tugging. In these cases you are looking for a small interest – literally, a grasp at the chaser tug-toy – that's all you need to build on. When the dog does show interest, try to refrain from touching the toy. Instead touch the dog. Praise, fuss, stroke and cuddle him so that he begins to understand that you aren't going to snatch the toy from him.

When he is comfortable with this, touch the toy and tug lightly. This is what I call a 'tiny tug'. Then let go and repeat the fuss and praise. You want the dog to be totally comfortable with your presence while he has the toy. This will also help when you move on to informal play retrieves (see page 155).

This assessment period is just that – and although I am mindful of what and how I reward – I do not see it as a priority.

Once I have established what the dog wants, I can start to manipulate this drive for what I want. From this initial session, I then plan my next session, making decisions as to how to interact with the dog and which skills I need to develop and work on.

THOSE THAT WANT TO TUG

If your dog has a high value for toys, the next challenge is harnessing that energy and drive – and ensuring he does not run off with the prize. The most common mistake when introducing tug is not allowing the dog to 'win' his toy on a regular basis. It is great that he has the drive to chase and grab the toy, but we want him to build the desire to bring it back. In order to achieve this, the dog has to feel comfortable, and unthreatened, when he has the toy. When I play tug, I want the dog to focus on me, pushing the toy into me, and engaging with me.

The dog needs to trust that you are not going to 'steal' his toy.

I allow him to 'win' the toy which helps to encourage him.

I then give him lots of close contact affection while he holds on to his prize.

If I am working with a 'green' tugger, I would let him win and then encourage him to hold the toy while I interact with him, cuddling him, praising him and stroking him. I want him to be confident that I am not going to snatch the toy from him. I work on building his sense of trust so that he values the interaction as part of the engagement.

To test this, I move away and see if he will actively pursue me in order to continue the interaction. Once I can see this happening, I try throwing the toy away to see if he will pick it up, and return to me for more interaction.

When the dog is tugging confidently, I move the game to different locations and try a variety of tugs – plastic bottles, tea towels, hosepipes, bit of rope – anything goes! You want to create drive for as wide a spectrum of toys as you possibly can, as this will allow you options in your training.

You may need to be tactful in the early stages so your dog trusts you will not steal his prize.
Photo: Juliet Dearbergh

Golden Rules for Establishing Tug

When you are playing tug, there are some points regarding how you should engage, and what you are looking for:

1. The dog should be in the moment; he should be attempting to pull the tug from you. If he is pretending to tug, or appears half-hearted, snatch the tug from him. Then tease him so when he does bite, you will get more intensity.
2. Mix up your body language: be strong, be passive, be active, and be weak. Be aware of your dog and adapt accordingly.
3. This is a simple rule I learnt years ago: 'I have it, you have it, we share it'. Depending on the strength of your dog's tug, adapt these factors into what is appropriate for him.
4. Add motion – zig zag away from your dog – and chase. Start off gently and build up.
5. Touch and tease your dog so that he wants the tug.
6. Remember the tug is prey; prey isn't going to give up without a fight. When the dog grabs the tug, small jerks at the tug can trigger him to bite down harder.
7. Once you have drive for the tug, try and prise it away from him, which will help to increase drive.
8. When building tug, keep it short and sweet. Tugging is physical, so be patient.
9. You want your dog weight shifting and trying to pull the toy from you. If he lacks confidence, go with any tiny effort he makes.
10. Miss-bites – when the dog just fails to grab the toy – are a great way to increase drive, but the timing of when you create a miss and when the dog gets to win is vital. Ensure that you time it just as he is really digging in and trying to get the tug.

JESSIE'S STORY

I am the world's worst 'fosterer' – I have failed with every foster I have taken on and ended up keeping every one of them! One of my failed fosters was a small, black Labrador bitch called Jessie.

Jessie was a dog that was 'looking for a home', and she came to me for fostering. I said I would help to find a home – but she had her own ideas, and she chose me. She was a sweet working type Lab; her previous owners had shown no interest in playing tug or even ball with her. When I got her, she was hand shy and nervous so my first priority was to build her confidence and to establish a relationship. I have found that one of the best ways of doing this is through play.

However Jessie didn't play – she had no desire to tug a toy. She loved to search for tennis balls, but she had no interest in bringing them back. If I tried to approach her, she would drop the ball and back off, waiting for me to pick it up and throw it again.

So my first issue to work through was her reluctance to bring the ball back. This is where training in a small space helps. I use the bathroom or kitchen when I am working on initial behaviours as these rooms are small, with minimal distractions, and it is relatively easy to manipulate the environment.

I began working on getting Jessie to feel comfortable with me being near her while she held a ball. I did this by throwing the ball, then keeping my hands away from it. I would move closer to her but if she dropped the ball I backed off. In a short space of time, she would hang on to the ball while I walked close by.

Next, I started to move my hands. This made her drop the ball instantly, but I just ignored the drop and waited for her to pick it up again. When she did I would make a big deal out of it, giving her lots of verbal praise.

I then progressed to fussing her while she held the ball. Luckily for me, Jessie was incredibly affectionate and loved physical interaction with me. I eventually got her to carry the ball, and allow me to be near her, and cuddle her, while she held it. I then stroked around her face and head, and she still hung on to the ball. When she was confident with this, I progressed to 'tiny tugs' of the ball. This consisted of tapping the ball with my fingertips which, initially, prompted Jessie to drop it. I simply waited for her to pick it up and then repeated the verbal praise and affection.

In time, I got to the point where Jessie would hang on to the ball while I tapped it. I built this up until I could tug with her on the ball. This was a huge milestone!

After that I progressed to tying the ball to a string and using that to initiate play. This went better than the initial stages, so I quickly moved on to a new toy. Jessie had built value for carrying toys around the house by this point, so I would repeat the 'tiny tug' stage with whatever she had picked up. Over time, Jessie gained more and more confidence in the game. I changed locations throughout my training and added more and more articles. Jessie's tug became so strong that I was eventually able to teach her to tug a bite-work sleeve, which she did with complete gusto and verve. She loved the game and this proved, more than anything, that play can be developed and built, even with the most unpromising start.

Tug can take months, or years to build to the level where it is valued by the dog. So be patient, do the work and don't rush.

SHAPING PLAY

This approach is for the extreme type of dog that has little prey drive, or has had a negative experience of playing tug. It is also useful for handlers who lack confidence in building play.

Some handlers truly believe that that their dog will not, or cannot, play. This is not the case; reluctance to play is merely a bump in the road that you can overcome. All you need to do is revise your approach and tactics and try again. Be subtle in your approach and don't expect too much, too soon. Play needs to be built and nurtured. Don't expect a dog that has a strong history of not interacting with rewards to start tugging like his life depends on it. Remember, it's about the journey not the destination – so enjoy it!

Once I have assessed or created food drive in a dog, I am ready to build play drive for a tug, a chase and a play retrieve. To progress to this stage, you need to:

- Ensure your dog has some experience of free shaping and is fully charged up to a clicker or clicker word.
- Ensure he also has an understanding of 'Itsyerchoice' (IYC). This is a system pioneered by Susan Garrett, which uses food to teach impulse control. For more information see page 133.
- Pick a time when your dog is most likely to be fully awake and aroused.

Just before mealtimes would be ideal.
- Prepare the food; I use high-value food that retains it shape and can be secreted in a toy if necessary. Small pieces of cheese or steak are ideal.
- Find a low level training environment, with no distractions.

SESSION I
To create drive for a toy, I use a chaser tug, made of soft fleece material. The reason will become apparent as you progress through the stages:
- I start the session exactly as I would when I do the initial assessment (see page 65), casually producing the toy and attempting to gain the dog's attention.
- To begin with, I wait for the dog to show any sign of interest in the toy or, better still, engage with it. I then click, or mark with my clicker word, and reward by feeding from the toy. I deliberately feed on the toy, pushing the treat into the material so the dog has to forage, mouthing and chewing on the toy.
- I repeat this several times and end the session. I am not looking for tugging, or any specific behaviour at this stage. I just want the dog to show general interest in the toy.

SESSION II
Starting where I left off, I am now looking for consistent acknowledgement of the toy.
- When the dog is showing an interest in the toy, I withhold the click, which will cause him minor frustration. This should prompt him to mouth, lick or, hopefully, bite the toy. I click this and set this behaviour as my criteria for reinforcement.
- When the dog makes contact with the toy, I don't attempt to tug it or instigate any sort of play. The biggest mistake people make when they are trying to create play/prey drive is expecting too much, too soon.
- I work on the assumption that a dog is not going to play so I will need to build and create real drive and desire for the reward. This ensures that I tread carefully; it prevents me from wading in and inadvertently offending the dog, which could put him off for life.
- Once the dog is consistently grabbing at the toy to get a reward, I start to build a tug. Up to this point, I have not touched the toy whilst the dog has been engaging with it. I simply reward any interaction with the toy by feeding on it.

I now start to move the tug while the dog is engaging with it. Again this needs to be done cautiously, especially if your dog is very sensitive. If you suddenly pull the toy away, this could be perceived as punishment. So when I first move the toy I try to be sneaky, dragging it away very slowly. I pull the toy far enough away so that I can then make a sudden movement. The reason for this is to see if the sudden movement incites a chase. If it does, I allow the dog to catch the toy, click, and reward from the toy.

SESSION III

I am now ready to progress the game in order to increase the dog's desire for the toy:

- When the dog is engaging with the toy – biting or chewing it – I snatch it away. I am careful to give a very weak pull as I don't want to deter him from chasing the toy. I always go in at a very low level of physical force when I pull, touch or tug, as I don't want to overpower him, and put him off playing. I want to condition that he wins the toy, and that he is successful in attaining his prize.
- Once you have created a tug, it is a case of building it by increasing the strength of the tug, the physical pressure you exert and the speed of movement. Being aware of your own body language, and the subtle messages you are conveying when you play, will also assist you. I try to make my body weak and floppy, letting the dog drag me about. My long term aim is to have a dog that will hang on to the toy regardless of the physical pressure I have on the reward. This will be built up over a period of time.

Humans and dogs use play to exercise, educate, stimulate and bond with each other. Utilising play into your training will not only improve your dog's behaviour, it will also enhance your relationship.

Top Tips for Reluctant Tuggers

1. Keep your session short. Seconds are better then minutes at first.

2. Think laterally about tugging; use bottles, hosepipes, fleece tugs, etc. Household objects, such as tea towels, make great tugs, so use your imagination.

3. Pick moments when your dog is excited: before a walk, when you are prepping his food, before you let him off the lead, etc. Look for when your dog is aroused and try tugging then.

4. You can click and reward tug with food games (see Food circuits, page 141). However, make sure you are getting what you want before rewarding. You are looking for real, engaged tugging.

5. Try using a food pouch or sock with food concealed in it. This is a great way to start tug – but make sure you get rid of the food as soon as you can.

6. Movement is your friend, so make the tug irresistible. This doesn't mean running around; it is how you present the tug that is key.

7. Don't become desperate; some dogs take time to become confident tuggers. If you pressure your dog into tugging, you could put him off.

8. Jealousy is a great way to create want. Ask someone to hold your dog on a lead, or put him in a crate while you are playing (or pretending) to play with another dog. Then be quick to get your dog and engage with him. If he switches off, just use the 'second' dog again.

9. Don't rush in to grab the tug from your dog. Let him win it and possess it. He has worked hard to 'kill' the prey so let him savour the moment.

10. Allow your dog to dictate the game, and let him pull you around. Start with tiny tugs, and build in duration as his confidence – and desire – grows.

Chapter Six

DEFINING GOALS AND TEACHING NEW BEHAVIOURS

D o you know what you want? No, I mean do you know what you really, really want? Surely there's a song in there somewhere…. But let's stay focused!

Heels, trainers or shoes – what do you want?

This seems like a straightforward question but when asked, it prompts a variety of responses.

If you were going to buy a pair of shoes, you would consider several factors before going out to the shops or searching the internet. You may think about what they are needed for. Casual? Formal? Budget? Colour? Waterproof? Size? Shape? The decisions you make may be affected by past experiences, speaking to friends, Google searches, learnt experiences, etc.

All these decisions will make for a shorter, more efficient, shopping trip; you will not will not waste time looking in the wrong shops, or waste money buying the wrong shoes or being distracted by some tempting offer.

I appreciate that sometimes an unplanned, impulse buy can be an excellent purchase. However, was it a genuine fluke that you got what you wanted? Or did you subconsciously go to the right shop where there was a high chance you would find your item of choice?

Either way, it's all about decisions.

WHAT ARE YOU LOOKING FOR?

When you are starting to train a behaviour, you need to consider what you want in exactly the same way as if you were planning an important purchase. What do I want? What do I want it to look like? What does it need to do? How strong do I want it to be? How fast do I want it to be?

These are all decisions that should be made at the outset. The tendency to make decisions as you go along is akin to throwing mud at a blanket and hoping that something sticks.

Surely, the quicker, faster route to a successful purchase would be to make those decisions before you even leave the house? In the context of training, making decisions before you start will save time, effort and energy, and will ensure that your forthcoming training sessions are structured, focused and goal orientated.

When you are training you should have always have a picture of your end goal in sight.
Photo: Chris Parkin.

If you have a clear picture in your head of what you want the end product to look like, you will minimise potential errors and optimise opportunities to reward and shape what you want.

This is where you can let your imagination run wild! You can be as vivid and specific as you like. What do you want your retrieve to look like? How tightly do you want your dog to turn? What do you want from your start line position? All these details need to be considered and your training formulated accordingly.

Think of Bob Bailey's famous mantra: 'think, plan, do, review'.

MAKING A PLAN

I am a big planner; I like to have a plan for

everything, be it making a coffee or training my dogs. It gives me the ability to know where I am heading and, more importantly, to be prepared if something goes wrong.

I start off with a clear idea for each training session. I do this mentally, but it may help to write it down and tick off each thing when you have done it. Go in with plan A, plan B and plan C! You also need to prepare for the times when things go wrong. You are working with a living animal so you need to expect the unexpected. The better prepared you are, the more likely you are to succeed and make progress.

I spend more time thinking about my training, than training itself. Ironically, this means that I train more efficiently and effectively because I have done all the 'training miles' in my head. I have made all the mistakes, or tried all the variations well before my dog is even in the equation or, sometimes, even born!

When I am getting a puppy or a new dog, I always set myself a challenge. I do this mainly because, after training lots of dogs for so many years, it's invigorating

Training Toolbox

In order to develop as trainers we must constantly learn and evolve. I look at each idea and technique I use as a tool. The more tools I have in my training toolbox, the better equipped I will be to deal with any malfunctions that crop up – and, trust me, they will. It is inevitable.

There is no handler who could look back on their dog's career and say, with complete honestly, that they made every correct decision and never encountered a problem. If you can, then you are one in a million!

Training is about learning; you may use one idea with your present dog, then not use it again for your next three. However, when your fourth dog comes along – and the same problem rears its ugly head – you can go into your toolbox, dust off that old tool/ idea and use it. The more you know, the better you will be able to determine what will and won't work. Remember to think it through first and don't just try something for the sake of it. Read your dog and be willing to adapt.

to change things and see what I can improve on, or refine, both for myself and for my students. Can I change something in my training to improve, experiment or question what I do?

Some of the challenges I have set myself include:

- Solely using a clicker.
- Solely using a verbal marker.
- Training without a clicker or a verbal marker.
- Training a dog with the minimal amount of training to achieve the same end result. For example, it took me less then 15 minutes to train Scooter and Thriller to perform a full competition retrieve, whereas this would normally take weeks to achieve.
- Solely using shaping (waiting for the dog to offer a behaviour).
- Solely using luring (guiding the dog to perform the behaviour).

The conclusion I have drawn from my experiments is that shaping is by far the most effective way to teach a dog a behaviour, and only the minimal amount of luring is needed before you progress to shaping. Don't get me wrong; I am not averse to luring. However, the problem comes when a handler gets stuck with luring for way too long. If I choose to use a lure, it's done for the minimal amount of times necessary, and I am deliberate and strategic in where and how I use it. The line between lure, target, and prompt can be grey. For example, a 'food follow', where the dog trots underneath the handler's out-stretched hand in heelwork training is both a lure and a target.

However, your strategy should always be for your dog to offer a behaviour, and then you can reinforce it.

Studies have also shown that shaping causes a dopamine release in the dog's body which results in a 'feel good' factor to shaping and therefore learning.

PAIRING BEHAVIOURS

When the ground breaking notion of component training – breaking an exercise into smaller pieces and teaching it in segments – was first introduced, the trend was to optimise the use of word recognition when teaching a new behaviour.

A dog would be induced to sit, either by luring or waiting for him to offer the behaviour, and then the word 'sit' would be continually repeated while the dog maintained this position: "sit, good sit, good, that's a good sit," etc.

So is this effective? You could argue that it is. Pairing the word with a behaviour allows for the association to be built, and for the dog to eventually understand that this is what he should do when he hears this verbal cue again.

However, let's look at it more analytically.

- First, is the verbal cue "sit" necessary when the dog doesn't perform this behaviour? Or to be more crude, why say it if you haven't got it yet?
- Is the cue "sit", an 'action' word, e.g. move into that position, a 'stay there' word, or both? If it is both, are both elements of the behaviour being offered?
- What are you going to do if the dog doesn't sit on cue? Will you 'punish' him? If so, are you sure he has sufficient knowledge of the word to warrant it? Have you gone through the process of generalising and proofing the behaviour? If your dog ignores the cue, what are you teaching him? That ignoring a cue is acceptable? So what happens when it really matters? Are you telling him that it's ok to ignore the cue in that situation?
- Is the behaviour exactly what you pictured in your mind? If this is not the case, why put a label on it and name it? A slow sit, a sloppy sit, a sit without attention? A sit and move? Again, what are you going to do if the dog doesn't meet your criteria for the sit, e.g. fast and crisp, as you have now named it?

All the above questions are relevant to this discussion.

So what do we know? We know that dogs are masters of body language, and will pick up on the tiniest of cues from our body rather than verbal cues. So why not use this to our advantage? Why not cue the behaviour with your body first – a suggestive head twitch or an arm held in a certain place – go through the process of refining, shaping, proofing, and then name it. Name it when you have the wow factor! Name it when you have the sit so pretty and sharp you want to shout it from the rooftops and tell the world! Why name it in the early stages when it isn't anywhere near what you want?

PUTTING BEHAVIOURS ON CUE

How hard is it to put a behaviour on a verbal cue? Well, consider this. You have the perfect sit being offered to you when you cue it with your body language. You can test it and guarantee that it happens.

Now, just before you anticipate the 'sit' is going to happen, you give the verbal cue. Boom! The dog does the exact behaviour you want – and all the gates open

Name it when you have the wow factor!

to reinforcement city! Can you imagine the dog's reaction to hearing that word 'sit'? You've got it! You have now labelled brilliance and the dog has nothing but positive associations with the word, and total understanding of what you want. If he does fail, the gates to reinforcement city slam shut, and the dog is clamouring at the door to get back in.

The 'sit' is a simple behaviour, but the same applies with any other behaviour you shape. For example, your dog has learnt to sit on on a wobble cushion – and you want to put that specific behaviour on cue. This is where 'loving it like you made it' comes into its own. It is a vital part of putting a behaviour on cue.

By now, your dog should be reliably offering the behaviour when the 'object' – the wobble cushion in this case – is presented. So every time your dog sees the wobble cushion he will be ready to sit on it – or perform any other behaviour you have specifically shaped on that item.

You may well have added criteria to the behaviour, such as remaining on the wobble cushion until you cue a release, or asking him to orientate himself in the direction you are facing.

Whatever you have decided you want for this exercise, you must ensure it is in place before putting a cue on the behaviour. Don't label it till you love it! You have shaped your dog to give you the response in exactly the way you want, and you are confident that he will repeatedly offer this response. This is what to do next:

- Start with presenting your object, and doing a few warm ups of the behaviour you are aiming for. Don't 'click' these, just give your dog a reward.
- Now pick up the object and say your verbal cue just a second before you place it on the ground.
- The dog should automatically offer you the behaviour you have just rewarded.
- You can now click this response.
- Once you have clicked the dog for giving you the behaviour after the verbal cue, you should no longer reward any unsolicited attempts. This is known as putting the behaviour under stimulus control. The dog learns that the window of opportunity to earn reinforcement is only open when he hears the verbal cue.

Once you have the behaviour on cue, you can progress to putting the behaviour on a variable schedule of reinforcement and shape more repetitions for one reward. This is the beginning of putting your behaviours in sequences or chains (see Chapter Ten: Chaining Behaviours).

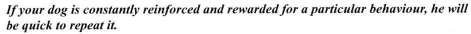

If your dog is constantly reinforced and rewarded for a particular behaviour, he will be quick to repeat it.

Chapter Seven

TO PUNISH OR NOT TO PUNISH?

R ight, lets put it out there! That dirty little word we hate to hear, use or see! Punishment!

The word 'punishment' instantly conjures up pictures of dogs being inhumanely and brutally chastised for simple and involuntary behaviour; it evokes an emotional response and divides dog trainers. In terms of our training conversation, it is the most emotive, confusing, controversial and misunderstood term.

As a reinforcement based dog trainer, do I use punishment? The simple answer is yes. I, Kamal Fernandez, international seminar presenter, top level dog sports coach, dog owner and dog lover, use punishment.

There it is in black and white, and at this point you could choose to leave the conversation and shut the door on anything I have to say or do, and that would be your choice.

Or you could listen to the full answer and make your own decision.

WHAT IS PUNISHMENT?

First we need to define 'punishment' in terms of the science and remove the emotional aspect. Punishment and reinforcement are terms that describe the effect on the behaviour. Punishment decreases behaviour and reinforcement increases behaviour. The terms 'positive' and 'negative' refer to whether we are adding or removing something.

Punishment has the effect of reducing the likelihood of a behaviour occurring. The aim of punishment is to weaken a behaviour, which may result in another, more desirable, behaviour emerging, which can then be reinforced.

Those of us that use reinforcement and,

I am an ardent dog lover – and, yes – I do believe there is a place for punishment as long as the terms are very clearly defined.

specifically, positive reinforcement, do so largely because we want to be nice to our dogs.

This is the most basic and simplistic dog training. We have made a conscious decision that we want to utilise methods and approaches that are 'nice'. We want to avoid any 'nasty' things if at all possible.

However, we would all agree that some of the choices a dog makes are so inappropriate that, despite the profuse levels of reinforcement, management and testing we have done, he still opts for the 'bad' choice. It happens, dogs are dogs. Sometimes temptation is too great to resist.

WHAT ARE THE OPTIONS?

So for those of us that are committed to using reinforcement, the question is what do we do in this situation? Is being 'mean' or 'nasty' the only option?

Let's take a look at the following example to find a way forward:
We understand that a consequence to our action – be it positive or negative –
can and should have a direct result on the outcome of the subsequent behaviour.
A dog that receives a treat every time he sits will inevitably find it beneficial to
sit. So what do we do when the dog doesn't sit?
1. Should we physically correct him for disobeying the cue?
2. Should we ignore his disobedience in the hope that it's a one-off?
3. Do we wait for the dog to respond and reward him?
4. Do we withhold the reward?

All the above are options; you could try one and get a response. But which is
likely to be the most effective? Let's take a closer look at the options and, using our
inner moral compass, we can gauge what is appropriate for a particular situation.
1. *Physical punishment*
   This isn't an option as far as I am concerned. I don't believe in hitting,
   smacking, grabbing, or forcing a dog into position if he doesn't do as I ask.
2. *Ignoring it*
   Top animal trainer, Bob Bailey has a fantastic saying: "reinforcement
   builds behaviour". I love it! It constantly reminds me of the core principle
   of reward-based training and the importance of rewarding. So, ignoring
   what we don't want and rewarding what we consider desirable is a brilliant
   option to implement. In the early stages of learning, I would definitely do a
   lot of ignoring of 'stuff' I don't want.
3. *Waiting it out*
   Waiting for the correct choice and rewarding will allow you to build value
   for the behaviour and thus increase the history of reinforcement. This will
   also get your dog to 'want' to do what you consider desirable.
      For example, if I am training a sequence in distance control and my
   dog doesn't do the position I have asked for, I can ignore it, give another
   position and then try the sequence again. This allows me to reward with a
   lower level reward before trying until I get the instant response, which I can
   reward with a high level reward.
4. *Withholding the reward?*
   Once I feel my dog knows the task, the most severe form of punishment I

would use is to deny the opportunity to earn reinforcement. If the dog has had a strong history of reinforcement for the correct behaviour, and his learning has been proofed and generalised, he should have a full understanding of what I am asking for.

So if he makes an error, the consequence would be that he doesn't get his reward. Harsh, I know!

That's right, the dog isn't going to get his piece of cheese, ball or tug toy. That's as bad as it gets!

So why does it work? It works because I have built up such a strong desire for the reward that not getting it will really hit home. It would be like handing out £50 notes to you, for weeks and weeks, in return for cups of tea. Then, one day there was no cup of tea – so no £50. Can you imagine how you would feel? Fundamental to this strategy is that the dog wants the reward. If I had used a lower value reward, would the dog be bothered that he didn't get it? Or if the dog had only been rewarded for that behaviour a few times, would he understand that it had value?

Punishment is not effective as a teaching tool as it doesn't build value for what you want. So how many wrong choices could the dog make? How long is a piece of string! Saying what you want is far easier then trying to eliminate all the things you don't want.

Effective 'punishment' should, therefore, be used to refine choices and work on detail. It should be used to polish existing behaviours not elicit new ones.

TIME OUT

Withdrawing the reward is best understood as a time-out for the dog. I might stop playing the game with my dog for a second or two. It may be that I end my session and stop altogether. It may be that I walk off and make the dog jealous by training, and rewarding another dog, or it may be that I hold his collar for 15 seconds. I find it helpful to divide my time outs into two main types:

1. I use the first variation to build desire in the dog so that he wants to complete the task I have asked for. So, if I ask my dog to sit and he fails to co-operate, I would openly play with the reward myself and have a 'party for one'. I have played this game in foundation training, so the dog recognises this as information. My aim is to lift the dog, and frustrate him, so that he tries

harder. The reward should be held out of reach so the dog cannot get to it. After baiting him in this way, I would then ask for the behaviour again. In this situation, I may get another dog out and ask for something I can reward, or I may freely give him the reward.

2. The second type of time out is more severe; it should be kept to a minimum and employed strategically. I would use it when my dog made an error and and I was totally confident that he knew the behaviour, had a long history of reinforcement for the behaviour, and the choice to not do the behaviour was clear to me. In this scenario, I would act as though the dog has disappeared. I may use this time to do some personal grooming or to look into the great blue yonder. I am effectively ignoring my dog and giving a very clear visual cue that I am not rewarding him. Additionally, I am withdrawing my attention as potential reinforcement. I may even put the dog away and get out another dog to train as a consequence.

Now there are a few caveats for each of these options:
- The behaviour needs to have been profusely reinforced and fully understood.
- The dog has to want to be present in the game and engage with me.
- The dog will dictate what is punishment and what is reinforcement.

If you observe the above caveats, these options of punishment will have an effect. Without each of these being considered, my use of 'punishment' will be ineffective.

Time outs are effective if used mindfully and carefully. They are still a form of punishment, so applying them should be done with that well-used mantra 'think, plan, do, review'. Whenever I reinforce a behaviour or a chain of behaviour, I constantly evaluate what I rewarded, where, when, how and why. The same attention to detail should apply to time outs.

The recent conscious change in training to reward based methods has been a positive step in dog training. However, there is a danger in becoming complacent with regards to using times outs over physical punishment. Yes, it is infinitely preferable – but how are you using them, and how frequently do you resort to them?

All training should incorporate an element of self-awareness and reflection.

A time out is a simple but effective method of withdrawing your attention and pointedly not rewarding your dog.

This is the only way we develop and move forward as trainers. This applies to the use of reinforcement and punishment. Punishment should be used strategically, if at all, and only on trained behaviours with a long and substantial history of reinforcement.

IS PUNISHMENT NECESSARY?

Some of you may read this chapter and ask, does this type of 'punishment' work or some may ask, is punishment necessary?

For dogs trained with choice, and with the opportunity to think, having consequences to their actions is almost inevitable. Being allowed to experiment with what does and doesn't receive reinforcement is, in itself, part of the process.

However punishment has a fall out. If the handler, or the dog, believes he is 'bad' it can create anxiety and stress. This is something that is greatly misunderstood in dog training. The point I would like to emphasise is that I am not punishing my 'bad' dog, I am explaining that his incorrect choice or behaviour was not appropriate.

There is a huge difference in those two perspectives. Punishment should be the last option, only used when there has been established learning, confidence building, and clear understanding. A no-reward marker should be trained as diligently as a clicker word or marker.

PUNISHMENT V REINFORCEMENT

I like to take on two puppies/young dogs quite close together, normally different breeds and different genders. When I got Punch, my male Boxer, and Fire, my female Border Collie, I set myself a challenge to see if I could remove all punishment from my dogs' lives – both in their formal training and in a domestic setting.

I had eradicated compulsion and physical correction from my training years ago so that wasn't a challenge for me. With Punch and Fire, I wanted to see if I could truly eradicate the use of any form of punishment. So no time outs, no response cost, no withholding reinforcement. Nothing. I have to admit that I failed, and here is how and why.

When dealing with any behavioural problem, your options are to manage, to train against and sometimes to ignore. The option you use is dependent on the situation and severity of the behaviour, and where it sits on your list of priorities.

FIRE FIGHTING REACTIVITY

Fire, my Border Collie, is from all working lines; she has a brilliant temperament but has always been incredibly motion sensitive. Her challenge was always going to be that she would develop reactivity triggered by motion.

When she was as young as eight weeks, she exhibited a strong desire to herd and chase. I vividly recall the first time I took her out for a walk with one of my other dogs. She took off on an outrun as fast as her legs could carry her, she headed the other dog and then stalked him as though she was at the International Supreme Championships and he was an obstinate ewe. Needless to say, she was allowed to rehearse this behaviour and played numerous games which channeled her desire to chase on to me.

There are some behaviours you can't afford to ignore, so I had to form a plan to counteract Fire's chase drive.

She was social with dogs and people, and even though she was a poor eater she had an inclination to resource guard when dogs approached her food. Her 'guarding' was mild at most. Given that she never took it any further than a growl, and I could manage this behaviour, I didn't overly invest time on it. Once she hit maturity she stopped of her own accord.

She was easy to mix with other dogs, being respectful yet confident. Friendly, but not rude. However she was sometimes so friendly that she would want to appease dogs and people. I trained against this by working on her recall and focus around, and near, other dogs. I put the opportunity to 'say hello' and engage with other people on cue. She was given permission to 'say hello' when she showed me calm and controlled behaviour.

At six months, while training with a friend, her chase issue reared its ugly head once more. We were doing restrained recalls, rotating amongst a small group of us. Initially, Fire was aware, but not overly interested, in the other dogs moving. However by the third recall, she couldn't restrain herself any longer. She lunged forward, screaming and barking at the dog moving. She was hysterical!

I immediately stopped what I was doing, and walked her away from the area. I tried to instigate some play and interaction, but she was gone. Her head had blown and I couldn't get any sense from her. So I put her in the car and formulated a plan. This was not something I was prepared to manage or ignore, as I knew what the long term ramifications would be. If this issue is ignored with high drive dogs, it can quickly escalate into a lifetime of management or, worse still, aggression.

I didn't put Fire in a situation where she was likely to repeat this behaviour until I had her focused and could rely on her total engagement. I worked on pairing all her chase drive into me, and worked her in environments with minimal distraction. I employed friends to assist me, gradually introducing more and more distractions and motion. If left and ignored, this could have easily escalated into a lifetime with a dog that was hysterical and out of control around anything that was fast moving. By dealing with this issue before it became a problem, I now have a dog that can be walked around an agility show oblivious to the temptations, and giving focus when needed.

So I managed Fire's chase drive and ignored her food guarding.

PERFECT PUNCH

Punch, my Boxer, was a very different type of dog in every way. He was the perfect puppy; he seemed to have an old soul and never did typical puppy things. He never chewed, he never made a mess in the house, he could be left unattended and would just lie quietly, often watching what was on TV. I called him 'perfect Punch.'

The initial part of his upbringing was trouble free. He was a docile, easy-going pup. He would mix with other dogs respectfully and wasn't exposed to any negative experiences. Everything was going swimmingly until we reached that testing time of adolescence. This is the time when your previously sweet, amenable little darling turns into a brat with horns coming out of his head! Lost recalls, lack of concentration, overly sexual behaviour are just some of the tell-tale signs that your dog has hit the teen years.

The first sign that Punch was a teen came when, in the space of a week, he was 'attacked' by three different dogs. These dogs were on our regular walking route and he knew them well. He had met them, played with them and interacted with them frequently. However, on all three occasions, Punch was the victim of unprovoked aggression from all three dogs.

What had changed? The reason was as clear as the nose on your face. Punch approached all three dogs in a way that they felt was inappropriate; he was being a rude teenager with his body language and intent. He didn't actually make contact with them on any of the occasions but, as a young male dog, he was emitting testosterone from his system which would have signalled like a red light about his head. The 'attacks' were at most scuffles – all flashing teeth and saliva. On each occasion, there was no damage or injury.

Coincidentally, the three dogs were all white. Two were smaller – a West Highland White Terrier and a crossbreed – the third dog was a large American Bulldog mix. All the dogs were male, and all were castrated.

Often castrated males can be the focus of an adolescent male dog's unwanted attention due to the lack of testosterone in their system.

Punch was clearly 'misreading' these dogs as his own hormones were running amok. This is a great example of a normal incident that could be the catalyst for creating a huge issue. On each of these occasions, Punch didn't show any sign of trauma or fear, but I was fully aware of the path it could take.

DAY OF RECKONING

Several weeks went by, and we had no further incidents. We also saw two of the dogs again, and Punch engaged with them in a more controlled situation, and there was no outcome. We went for a brief walk with both, and ended each session with the dogs off lead and interacting in a largely indifferent manner.

However when we met the large American Bulldog cross, he lunged, and barked at Punch, even though he was on lead and at a considerable distance.

Punch was off lead so I called him back and put him on a lead. He came back instantly, and we walked in the opposite direction. I reinforced Punch for being focused on me, and after a short distance, I let him off the lead and we resumed our walk. At this point, we heard the American Bulldog bark from some distance.

This wasn't directed at Punch, but he instantly tensed up, and looked in the direction of the other dog. I called him, and he ignored me. Up to this point, Punch had never ignored his name. His recall was 100 per cent in all environments and under all distractions. This was 'perfect Punch', remember? Well, he was about to tarnish his reputation.

As I stepped towards him, I was considering my options. I decided I would get him by the collar, and put him on the lead again. I wasn't in a position to deal with the situation, as I hadn't ever experienced it before. And I knew what I didn't want to happen...

Bear in mind, I had Fire at the same time as Punch. There was only six months between them, and she had been a more challenging puppy. She had an intense herding instinct and wanted to chase. I had used management and restricted her access to rehearsing inappropriate behaviour, and we had successfully come through her recall issues. It had taken careful planning, vigilance, plus a clear understanding of what I was trying to achieve. However Fire's triggers were easy to avoid on a day-to-day basis. She would get over-aroused by fast motion, my dogs, other people's fast moving dogs, agility, motion etc. I managed this on a daily basis, as I didn't expose her to these stimulants.

But, on this occasion, when I approached Punch, I knew that I hadn't anticipated this part of our journey. Up until this point, he hadn't shown any sign of aggression towards dogs.

He had been well socialised, mixing with a wide and diverse cross section of dogs in lots of environments, and he had great social skills. Punch took off towards the dog that had been barking at him. For a laid back, easy-going pup, he had suddenly found his 'inner' Greyhound! I tried calling him, and there was nothing. He was so intent on getting to the other dog, any attempt to use his name would have been in vain. Punch got to the other dog and instantly, without hesitation, tried to grab him. He was angry!

I set off in hot pursuit of him and, thankfully, my days of doing athletics paid off. As Punch launched himself, I was directly behind him and managed to grab him mid-air. I pulled him away, but he was still trying to grab the dog. Fortunately for me, the owner was most understanding, and took his dog away. He even apologised to me. In fact, neither dog had made contact, but if I had not intervened who knows what would have happened? I was absolutely mortified. Here I was, a professional dog trainer, attempting to tread the path of reinforcement-based dog training and I had a dog that ran ran off, ignored my recall cue and attacked another dog! Embarrassment, shame – these words did not come close to how I felt. I was only five minutes from home but the walk back seemed like hours.

I knew that I was at a crossroads. I could probably fix this issue by using compulsion – but that was not what I wanted. I didn't want to resort to using methods and approaches that I had long moved away from and, to be honest, I was not sure that they would be effective.

I had made a pact with myself to train these dogs without the use of punishment, and as this was the first problem I had encountered with Punch, I felt I should at least try to resolve it. I owed it to our relationship.

THE MASTERPLAN

So I formed a plan. I scrutinised every aspect of my relationship with Punch, and I was hypercritical.

These were my observations – and my plan of action:

- Punch had an excellent recall, but I needed to increase his arousal so that I could challenge his ability to complete this under extreme distraction. I needed to be vigilant and aware of every environment I put him in, and ensure that I was in control of what was going on, and that I had high value food or toys on me at all times.
- I wouldn't allow him to meet dogs that I felt might be contentious. That included other adolescent males, dogs with extreme fear, or those with poor social skills.
- I would feed the vast majority of his meals by hand, via training or interaction.
- I would ask for a 'please' or 'thank you' behaviour for everything he

wanted. So, for example, if he wanted to go off the lead, he had to offer a sit in order to be released.

- I would work on his focus around other dogs; initially at a considerable distance, and gradually edging closer.
- I would reinforce every behaviour, or appropriate interaction, he offered when he was around other dogs, whether it be by praise and a stroke or food. I would not take his good behaviour for granted,
- I would revisit socialisation, enrolling the goodwill of others to assist me with parallel walking, then free running if appropriate.

Very quickly, Punch's behaviour drastically improved. He started to re-focus on me and was less of a 'lager lout' and more of a 'gentlemen'. We were back on track, heading in the direction I wanted our relationship to go.

DISASTER STRIKES

I noticed that Punch had mild lameness on his front right leg when he was returning from a walk. At the time I wasn't overly worried; it was so minor that unless you really watched the dog you wouldn't have seen it. I was due to go to Canada for three weeks, and I had arranged for Punch to stay in kennels. This would be a perfect opportunity for him to rest and get sound.

While I was away I got regular updates saying that, even with rest, Punch was still showing signs of intermittent lameness. Some days he would be fine, and others he would appear stiff when he stood up, but then walk it off. Again, it was a minor niggle and nothing glaring. He was taken to the vet and painkillers were prescribed as standard.

On my return he was still not 100 per cent sound, although he appeared to be a little better. I decided to investigate further. I won't go into the whole story – it would fill the pages of another book in its own right. Let's just say it was a very challenging time.

We discovered that Punch had a supraspinatous tendon strain, which was at the root of his lameness. It took two years to diagnose, to treat – undergoing surgery – and then rehabilitate him. This involved varying periods of crate rest, coupled with pedantic rehab work.

By the time Punch was sound again, his behavioural work had suffered. At best it had been sporadic, and now I was faced with an entire, three-year-old male who was suffering from limited exercise and lack of stimulation. This coincided with Fire coming into season – so all my demons came to haunt me!

To make matters worse, I started to have major issues with Punch and my other male Collie, Super, which were exacerbated by the presence of an in-season bitch. Super was hitting adolescence and he and Punch were not seeing eye to eye at all. To say my domestic situation was fraught would be an understatement. My commitment to training with purely positive reinforcement was being severely tested.

Everything came to a head when Punch and Super had a major altercation. There was no injuries to either dog and, again, their interaction was largely superficial. But it put the whole house on egg shells. I was seriously questioning what I was going to do.

THE OPTIONS

When you have a situation like this, it's easy to feel overwhelmed and to think you have no options. I can empathise with people in this situation. My dogs weren't getting on, and the tension was unbearable.

Once again, I did some serious soul searching and went through all the options:

1. I could rehome one of the dogs. This is an option – but not one for me. While I don't judge people for feeling they have to rehome a dog, I just couldn't bring myself to do so. For me, it would be like rehoming a child.

2. I could manage the situation so the two dogs did not share living quarters. This would have been relatively easy to accomplish. However my dogs have always got on, and I wanted to reach this point again. I didn't want to live a life where the two dogs had to be kept in separate areas of the house. I know people do this, and they talk of the stress and tension it creates, the constant worry about doors being left open and dogs meeting. However, if need be, this would be a better option then rehoming.

3. Use aversives such as rattle cans, spray collars, or worse! Again, this is not an option for me. I would rather put up with the two dogs living in separate quarters.
4. Castrate Punch. This was a viable option, but what if it did not solve the problem? It could be that his behavioural issues were too ingrained to be resolved in this way.
5. A combination of various bits of the above.

Well, I choose the last option and worked out a strategy that involved segments from all the options.

PUTTING IT INTO ACTION

First I separated both dogs so that they lived in different areas of the house and they were never left together. I didn't want them rehearsing their behaviour so they weren't allowed together. I was able to section off our garden with fencing so they could be near each other, but without contact.

I had both dogs chemically castrated. This was a good halfway point to to see if it would actually help. At first, as is often the case, Punch got worse. However, after a brief time, his behaviour started to improve.

I also made a concerted effort to walk, feed and interact with both dogs together. This was always in a controlled manner and laden with reinforcement.

This is the point at which I did use punishment. I had been working for several weeks and they had been progressing to the point where I could feed them in crates near each other, and even give treats when they were near each other.

I decided it was time to introduce a ball throw. I asked for Punch to wait, whilst I threw a ball for Super. I kept this low key at first. I repeated the throw several times, then switched so Super had to wait whilst Punch had the ball thrown. This went really well until I finished the session, and went to release Punch. He instantly made a beeline for Super.

Luckily I had him on a lead. As he lunged, I made a loud nose. Punch had never heard me do this, and he stopped in his tracks. He looked visibly startled. He paused, and I praised him. As soon as my intonation changed, he headed back for Super. I repeated my loud noise. This time he stopped, looked back at me and froze. I instantly fed him numerous treats. I asked for a sit, and then rewarded again.

The look on Punch's face spoke volumes, he had never heard me react in this manner. In fact, it wasn't intentional – it was just a reaction to his behaviour.

This was a turning point in Punch and Super's relationship, and therefore in my relationships with them.

I took both dogs home and reviewed what had happened. Looking back, I don't think Punch 'knew' that his behaviour was not what I wanted. He was just reacting out of pure instinct. In that very moment where I made a loud noise, he realised I didn't like what he was doing.

It was his 'aha' moment. It was as if he was saying: "oh I get it... you don't want me to attack Super... why didn't you say so!"

I know this is anthropomorphising animal behaviour, but that's the only way I can describe it. Up until this point, I had made such an effort to reinforce Punch's good behaviour; I had socialised him, built up his confidence around other dogs and reinforced every good behaviour. When I highlighted that 'swearing' at your brother is not acceptable, he understood perfectly that I didn't like it.

Punch and Super's relationship went from strength to strength. So much so, that they are now together all the time. If two dogs are going to share a bed, it will be Super and Punch!

Punch is now the sociable, well-adjusted dog that I started with. Don't get me wrong, I am always aware that he is an entire male Boxer, and I assess every meeting, or potential meeting, with open eyes. That's not to say, I don't let him meet dogs – but I am always vigilant. I know that Punch is not a dog that will turn the other cheek, so I always ensure he has positive experiences. I never take his appropriate behaviour for granted. Still, to this day, I will reinforce him intermittently for appropriate behaviour around other dogs.

So was it punishment that solved the problem?

The answer is no. Reinforcement created a clear and concise picture of what I wanted. Then a loud noise, repeated twice, told the dog that I didn't

Finding the right reinforcement for your dog – and providing it in abundance – is the key to training success.

like his outburst, and then he was instantaneously back to a life filled with reinforcement.

My use of a loud noise was definitely a punishment, there's no doubt about it. But the only reason it worked so powerfully was because of the huge amounts of reinforcement around its use. I then only had to use it minimally and, within the spectrum of punishment, it was relatively moderate.

Punch was shocked by the reaction his behaviour provoked, and because it was used minimally, and in a planned and strategic manner, it had the desired effect. Because of the clarity with which it was done, there was no fall out. This is not usually the case with punishment.

Punishment used badly, or misused, can create long-lasting problems.

I believe that a large part of the catalyst was the enforced restrictions on Punch's life caused by his lameness. This was an exception to the norm of rearing a dog. Without this, I am sure he would not have needed the 'punishment' that led to a change in his behaviour. I also feel that with diligent exposure, and restrictions, to the dogs that he met, I could have avoided this.

This has drawn me to conclude, yet again, that reinforcement is the most appropriate approach. It can do so much of the work for you.

Be vigilant and be aware. Don't take your dog's good nature for granted. Live a life full of reinforcement so your dog always knows what you expect from him.

Chapter Eight

COPING WITH STRESS AND FRUSTRATION

The history of dog-human relationships has been one fit for a Spielberg movie: the story of taming wild wolves, incorporating them into our lives, befriending them, domesticating them, selecting and breeding them... raising them for a purpose – even if only to feature in a cute selfie!

Our paths have been intertwined for centuries, as has the process of training them. We have swung from extreme levels of punishment to more co-operative approaches, which take into consideration what dogs want and need. We have been influenced by science, and the knowledge gained from those that care for wild animals in captivity, to create a living environment that is comfortable, humane and ethical.

I, for one, am thankful to share ideas and knowledge – from any source – if it allows me to train more effectively and with increased clarity. However, we are a society that swings from one extreme to another.

There are two distinct words – or issues – that are becoming more and more contentious when mentioned in relation to dogs and their welfare and training.

The words are 'stress' and 'frustration'.

Before you start hyperventilating – hear me out!

A BETTER UNDERSTANDING

As training of dogs has become more reinforcement-based, so has the way in which we perceive and engage with our dogs. We are more aware of our responsibility towards them.

We understand the need to consider their ways of communicating, and their body language, something that was previously disregarded as being irrelevant.

At the same time, we have made the concepts of stress and frustration taboo subjects that can divide a roomful of dog trainers and behaviourists. However, in so doing, we have failed to understand how both these concepts can assist and help our dogs to be happier and healthier, and more accustomed to the world we ask them to co-habit with us.

Stress and frustration are not necessarily negative concepts – at least not in excess – and that is the key. Anything in extreme can be damaging: too much food can cause health issues, too much sun can cause cancer, too much rain can cause a flood. But all these things, in appropriate doses, are needed for us to lead normal, healthy lives. I see stress and frustration in the same light.

We expose our dogs to high levels of stress in the competition arena – but this can also be seen as a positive.

The world is full of situations and circumstances that will create stress and frustration, so failing to educate our dogs in how to deal with these emotions is preventing them from being healthy.

As a sports dog trainer, I can work and harness both stress and frustration to create better performance. I can teach my dogs how to think while in a heightened state of arousal, and how to cope with frustration.

But the process of inoculating a dog against stress and frustration is not for the sake of sporting achievement. It is because I want a dog that can function happily, safely and confidently in a world where he may experience both emotions on a daily basis, unpredictably and uncontrollably. He needs to develop and be taught coping tactics. That is my responsibility; it is no different than preparing my daughter for the same challenges when she grows up and faces the world.

The reluctance to understand and embrace the concepts of stress and frustration can be attributed to several factors.

I believe that we, as dog owners and trainers/behaviourists, feel guilty about the way we treated our dogs in the past. Our judgment, and the techniques and methodology we used, were lacking in compassion and understanding. I hold up my hand to this, but in this instance, I am not referring to individuals but to a collective industry. We have all made mistakes and misjudgments – that's part of the human experience. Fortunately we know better now, but could it be that we are over-compensating for our past guilt?

As mentioned previously, the influence on dog training and care by those who work with other species has been significant. It has raised our awareness in terms of management, enrichment and living with animals in environments that are not 'their own'. This has been a major revelation, and we can all put the knowledge that has been gained to good use.

However, there are additional factors to consider. Dogs and humans have a unique and deeply interwoven relationship, more so then most other species. That is not to discredit the close, interpersonal relationship others may share with their axolotl or arachnid, but we have literally created a species of animal that is custom-made for our needs. This, in turn, has affected the dog's ability to relate to us.

Each and every dog faces challenges, on a daily basis, as a result of this close inter-personal relationship in a way that does not apply to other species. This could be simple things like getting used to the sound of the TV or the vacuum cleaner, it could be interacting with children, meeting new dogs at 'their' park, or allowing strange people to come into 'their' house – the daily stresses we expect our dogs to cope with are endless.

And that is not to mention the unpredictable challenges they may face – an elevator, a hot air balloon, a reversing dustbin truck – unusual things, but any, if not all, could be encountered, without warning, on any single day.

PRACTICAL MEASURES

It would be brilliant if every dog had a sound, bombproof temperament but, often, this is not the case. We therefore need to take steps to make our dogs' lives as easy as possible. Strategically and systematically, we need to inoculate our dogs against stress and frustration to help them navigate their way through 'our world'. This means allowing them time to acclimatise to the world, to gain confidence and 'let them be' while they figure out what is going on and how they should respond.

Now before you throw up your hands in disgust, let me clarify. There is a huge difference between subjecting your dog to stress and frustration at a level that harms him emotionally, mentally or physically, and introducing him to challenges that may cause stress and frustration, but in such tiny doses he barely notices. The proviso is that you always provide reinforcement for overcoming the challenge, and always monitor your dog's level of confidence as a bench mark for progression.

It helps if you compare it with an exercise programme where you systematically stress your body so that it can adapt and become stronger. Rest days in between exercise are crucial, and you are realistic about taking time to build up your fitness. Equally, you would not try to exercise if you were ill or injured – this would be asking for trouble.

In terms of dog training, this would be the equivalent of exposing a fearful or anxious dog to additional stress and frustration – a sure way to shatter his confidence.

Shaping, adding arousal systematically, and creating achievable challenges for your dog, are just some of the ways to build his confidence and bolster it. Jackpots, thoughtful training and awareness will create a dog full to the brim with confidence who is ready to conquer the world.

Chapter Nine

REFINING REWARD AND REINFORCEMENT

My dogs live in a world of choices, and everything that they want is paired with behaviours that I want. This extends to reinforcement that goes beyond the obvious.

For example, my dogs all understand that they have to wait before coming out of my vehicle. This is trained initially with food and carries over from their crate training in the house. They understand that they have to wait for permission to come out of the crate.

When I start teaching a dog that he must wait before he comes out of my vehicle, I might reinforce him with a treat, or a game of tug, for coming out when asked. However this very quickly progresses to 'life reinforcements' like going for a walk, or getting to train or do other fun stuff with me. This fun stuff far outweighs the food and toys, so ensuring that I have control over these reinforcements is crucial.

Being aware of what your dog finds reinforcing is key to avoiding conflict and correction. So if your dog likes to swim, harness that desire so you can utilise it. If your dog likes to chase squirrels, harness it to teach a great sit stay. If your dog likes to tug, harness it to teach great focus and attention. Don't fight what your dog wants – use it! Use it to reinforce behaviours that you do want, rather then trying to combat his desires.

My dogs live in a world that is rich with reinforcement – and this allows them to make the 'right' choices.

CREATING DRIVE AND DESIRE

Drive and desire are generally regarded as inherited characteristics, based on a dog's breed, genetics and lineage. Undoubtedly, there is a lot of truth in this, but drive and desire can also be created, developed, nurtured, refined – and, indeed, ruined – by training.

Initially, the level and intensity may not be sufficient to use as a high value reward. However, it can be cultivated so that it becomes a reward, and a tool that allows you to bond and engage with your dog.

So how do you play with your dog in a way that elicits drive and desire, which can then be utilised to train and reinforce him?

When you play with your dog there are simple rules that you should consider:

- He has the toy
- You have it
- You both have it

The proportions you allow depend largely on the strength of the dog. For example, if I have a soft dog, I allow him to win the toy and possess it the

106

majority of the time. If I have a stronger dog, I can have more possession of the toy. You can also use it to instil confidence and self-esteem by allowing a less confident dog to 'win' more.

A strong dog can be controlled and channelled by games and a weaker, softer dog can be built up.

As a trainer that utilises reinforcement, you must always remain in the driving seat and have control of the rewards.

If the task becomes so self-rewarding that the dog no longer needs the rewards, how are you going to refine, improve or 'punish'?

Thought needs to be given to the type of reward – colour, material, size, shape – and how it will fall and move.

HIERARCHY OF REINFORCEMENT

Knowing what your dog loves, likes or doesn't mind in any given situation is key to being a mindful trainer. This is the equivalent of a 'top ten' of reinforcements in your dog's life. Be aware that this will change from environment to environment. So a number one reward in one situation may be a number ten in another.

Being aware of your dog's hierarchy of reinforcement will allow you to exploit his drive to get what you want. There are times when you want him excited and quick in his movements, other times you will want him sedate and thinking. Knowing what effect the reinforcement has on your dog will allow you to exploit his state of mind to your advantage.

What is reinforcement for your dog? You need to know the order of which is the most powerful, which is the least effective, and where the others fall in-between. Knowing what makes your dog tick will help you create the superstar you have always wanted!

Here is a 'top ten' list for 'Punch' at home:

1. Liver treats
2. Chicken
3. Cheese
4. Ball on rope
5. Praise, physical contact
6. Lead
7. Hard ball

8. Static food delivery
9. Moist dog treats
10. Kibble

Here is a 'top ten' list for Punch away from home:
1. Bite pillow
2. Fleecy tug
3. Raw food
4. Bite bar
5. Liver treats
6. Chicken
7. Cheese
8. Ball on rope
9. Praise, physical contact
10. Lead

Note that when we are away from home, some of the reinforcements that have value at home no longer feature on the top ten list.

REINFORCEMENT ZONE

Top agility trainer, Greg Derrett, refers to the 'reinforcement zone'. This is a turn of phrase I have adopted because it best captures the area/place where I want the most reinforcement to occur, which will help the dog to get the message as quickly as possible.

For example, if I am training a sit stay, the reinforcement zone would be at the dog's head height or above his head. This will encourage him to remain in the sit as the reinforcement comes to him in that position. If I was teaching my dog to go to a target set away from me, the reinforcement zone would be at the mat.

We know the importance of the 'click'. However it is equally, if not more important, to be mindful of what you do after the click. The side effects of having a weak reinforcement zone will, undoubtedly, lead to a variation in the behaviour, and by-products you may not want.

For example, you mark your dog for doing great heelwork, but then throw the reinforcement forward. This will result in the dog altering his position in anticipation of the reinforcement going forward.

In the initial stages of learning you want 80 per cent of your reinforcement to occur in that reinforcement zone. The remaining 20 per cent can vary. So if I was teaching a dog to wrap round a wing, for example, the majority of my reinforcement would be at the wing – in the reinforcement zone – the rest of my rewards could be positioned at a distance from the wing, either on the ground or coming from me.

Susan Garrett, uses the term 'transfer of value' when she is making a totally mundane, boring exercise, object or behaviour become the most important and exciting thing in the world.

The value of having a reward that means everything to your dog cannot be over-emphasised, as his desire for the reward will transfer on to the behaviour you are training. For example, if I asked you to go to work for £1, you would be reluctant and probably not think it was worth the effort. However, if I asked you to go to work for £1million, you would probably be salivating at the prospect!

It's no different with your dog. If every time your dog touched his dumbbell he was clicked and earned some steak, he would quickly transfer the value of the steak to the dumbbell, thus creating a dog that is salivating at the sight of a dumbbell.

Use your amazing rewards to teach things, as you are building a history of lots of value for doing that behaviour.

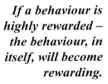

If a behaviour is highly rewarded – the behaviour, in itself, will become rewarding.

COMBINING FOOD AND PLAY

By this point you should be well on your way to having great play skills and great food skills, so now is the time to combine the two. This is where most people encounter problems.

So again, the process is simple but not easy. Being able to control your dog's mental state is crucial, and being able to affect his arousal is imperative.

There will be occasions when you want your dog to be more thoughtful and stoic rather than in drive and arousal. The type of reinforcement you use can create the 'right' mental state, so having a dog that will take anything you offer is worth investing in.

You will have identified whether your dog is toy/play motivated or food motivated. Depending on which it is, start with the dog's weakest preference. So, in the following example, my dog is toy motivated but not that into food. Fire, my Border Collie, is very much this type. She will often miss meals in day-to-day life, but will always take food in training because she has bought into the two-approach system.

APPROACH 1

The first approach relies on the Premack principle – using a preferred behaviour to reinforce a low value behaviour.

For example, if your dog loves tug and likes, but doesn't love, food circuits (see page 139), you can work these two together in the following way:

- Ask your dog to perform the low value skill, for example the food circuit.
- As soon as he completes this, mark the behaviour and use the high value reinforcement, i.e. a game of tug.
- When you ask the dog to do the low value behaviour again, he will probably get stuck. No problem, this is normal. Try again.
- If he still can't/won't/doesn't do the food circuit, take him further away from the high value reinforcement and try again. Distance is always an asset when working through distraction issues. You may have to lower criteria at first; a shorter distance is not so challenging.
- As soon as you get a response, mark and deliver the high level reward, i.e. a game of tug.
- The distance you have to move away from the high level reinforcement

will decrease as the dog understands that performing the low value behaviour is the key to getting the thing he wants.

APPROACH 2

For this approach, you need to rate your dog's skills in order of preference from most preferred to least preferred. You also need to identify whether your dog is primarily motivated by food or toys.

- If your dog is toy motivated, pick a game he least prefers. Then select the food he likes the most.
- Start with the game he likes the most, and reward with food.
- Switch to the least exciting game, and reward with a toy.
- Alternate between the two.

The key to this approach is that your dog must have some value for the games, even if it is minimal.

So for example, when I was working with Fire, I used food circuits, name games, and value for a dead toy (see Chapter 12: My Favourite Foundation Games) as a combination as she is movement orientated. As the food was linked to the more active game, she was happy to switch between the two.

Adapt this concept for your own dog, using a high value reinforcement to build value for a low value behaviour or a low level reinforcement.

ENDING ON A GOOD NOTE

Whilst teaching one of my regular groups, we started discussing whether you should reward your dog at the end of the session, irrespective of what he had been working on, or the relevance of that last reward.

The notion of leaving your training on a 'good note' is something that is often advised and still endorsed. Where does that expression come from? I remember reading an article written by international agility competitor, Silvia Trkman, who discussed this exact point, and I found her comments so insightful. She believes the concept came to fruition when training utilised more compulsive methods. So, you left the session on a 'good note' in the hope that your dog wouldn't remember the negative aspects of the session, and would come out next time with an upbeat attitude to training. I can definitely see how she reached that conclusion.

However, as a trainer, coach and teacher, who uses reinforcement based methodology, I still see handlers adhering to this concept – yet the people that I teach couldn't be further away from compulsive training if they tried. So why do people who subscribe to a reinforcement based system, feel the need to end their session on a good note? I believe there are several reasons:

1. Regardless of the sport or discipline you have chosen, dog training is a culture, and the cultural traditions and norms run through all facets of this. So ending your session on a good note is a concept that is cultural.

2. People who gravitate to a reinforcement based system of dog training largely want to reinforce their dog or, in more simplistic terms, be 'nice' to their dog. So if a session involves challenges and struggles, and maybe some degree of failure, and no reinforcement delivered, the moral obligation is to reward the dog at the end of the session, or to engineer the dog getting reinforcement. This is regardless of what the dog is learning.

3. Becoming casual in delivery of reinforcement, rather then being mindful and strategic. Again, the Bob Bailey mantra 'think, plan, do, review', resonates in my mind constantly and allows for mindful and purposeful training with intent, rather then casual practising or rehearsing.

4. Failing to acknowledge the effective and timely delivery of reinforcement as information. So, for example, if you pet your dog in an attempt to pacify him when he demand barks, you are actually reinforcing him for exactly the behaviour you want to stop.

Reinforcement based dog training heightens the need for clear, ultra-effective communication. As a crossover dog trainer, the awareness, thinking and analysis I now utilise, compared with how I initially trained dogs, is like night and day. Don't get me wrong, I have always been a trainer that 'thinks, plans and does...' but now I have to be aware of the smallest nuance of behaviour, placement of reinforcement, differential reinforcement, schedules of reinforcement, generalising the smallest detail.... the list is endless.

But for me, therein lies the joy. Initially it may seem overwhelming, but once that light switch is turned on, this approach to training seems entirely natural.

So the issue of not receiving a reward, or the specific reward the dog may want, isn't necessarily about being nice or nasty – it is information to the dog.

Therefore, ending a session and not getting his best toy, or his favourite food, is information to the dog. Even walking out of a competition ring and asking your dog to do an additional exercise before rewarding him, isn't being 'mean'. What you ask for would all depend on your dog's capability, whether his performance was average or better, and what schedule of reinforcement is attached to each behaviour/behaviour chain.

I am also very aware of classical conditioning, the importance of maintaining my dog's emotional response to training and the power of the dog wanting to play the game, so this concept should again be implemented with thought and consideration.

Don't feel you need to end a training session on a good note at all costs; withholding a top reward can be useful feedback for the dog.

So, the next time you want to end your training session on a good note, ensure the 'good note' is appropriate. Reinforcement builds behaviour, so you need to ensure the behaviour you are building is the behaviour you want.

Chapter Ten

CHAINING BEHAVIOURS

For the majority of you reading this book, the goal of your training is to compete in a dog sport – be it obedience, agility, heelwork to music, or working trials. For others, the aim is to have a well-behaved companion or family friend, or you may be involved in training assistance dogs, or maybe even police dogs.

No matter the differences in disciplines, you need to train your dog to undertake a series of single behaviours seamlessly, one leading into the other. The end goal is to have a happy, contented partner that lives to please, co-operates with every request and responds instantly to every cue you give.

Training dogs to perform a chain, or a series of behaviours, is no easy ask. Often with reward-based training, you get so immersed in perfecting the components that there is little or no chaining of the behaviours. The result is a dog that is unable to perform the larger exercise, or is missing vital elements.

So what is a chain? A chain or sequence of behaviour involves the following elements:

- **The complete picture:** This is the full test/exercise, as per your given rule, regulations or requirements. This would be in the real-life situation with distractions and external variables, such as a judge, steward, ring ropes/fences etc.
- **Linking exercises:** These are tricks or simple behaviours to keep your dog engaged and focused on the task at hand. Twist, spins, walk backs, through

Regardless of whether you are training your dog for a competitive sport, or as a well-behaved companion, there will be times when you need to teach a series of behaviours and then link them together.

your legs are all examples of linking exercises.

- **The individual exercise:** This is the individual exercise that makes up the test as per your rules or regulations. For example, retrieve, sendaway, heelwork, 20 elements on the agility field etc.
- **Components of the exercise:** These are the tiny bits that make up the complete exercise. The sit, wait, look, etc.
- **Single pieces of behaviour:** This is a breakdown of the bits of a component part. This may be a foot in a particular place, the drive for the reward, the speed, duration etc.

Each element has criteria which the dog must meet in order to earn his reinforcement. This has been pre-determined by the trainer, and shaped over a period of time, paying attention to criteria, rate of reinforcement, and timing.

115

STARTING THE CHAIN

If you want your dog to complete a single behaviour, you need to have a picture of what you want in your head before even attempting to train it. You then need to formulate a plan, or a route, of how you are going to attain this, and then orchestrate the environment so that the dog offers you a particular response.

You need to consider the type of reinforcement, the environment, the side effect of the reinforcement, and the position of the reinforcement/reinforcement zone.

Once you have decided what single behaviour you want to obtain, you then need to shape the quality and specifics of that behaviour. This is where you consider details such as speed, height, position and strength, to name but a few. This is where you stylise or 'pretty up' the particular behaviour, taking into consideration your personal preference, taste and goal.

The first step in creating a chain of behaviours is being unpredictable with when you reward your dog. At this stage you can start to select the better examples of the behaviour to click. For example, my dog may offer a sit and I may click him as it was a particularly good sit. He may then offer the behaviour again, and this time I may not reward it with food or a toy, and would just praise him. He may then offer a better response in an attempt to get me to reward him.

I would click and feed for this sit. I have started to tighten the screws on the type of sit I am prepared to reward. For example, I will only reward fast sits.

When I can reliably predict that this response will occur, I would add a cue. From this point, I would not reward my dog if he offered me this response, generally speaking.

This is a broad statement, but once a behaviour is on cue, I want the dog to understand that he stands the greatest chance of reinforcement occurring when I cue the behaviour. The window of opportunity to receive reinforcement is only open when I have the 'key' which is, in this case, a 'cue'.

The dog can choose to offer me a 'free' sit, but this would be unlikely to be reinforced.

You now need to generalise the behaviour and pay particular attention to trainer Susan Garrett's DASH principle: Desire, Accuracy, Speed, Habitat.

All these need to be monitored and considered.

Each piece of your chain needs to be trained as a separate component, which is then proofed and generalised. The phrase – 'you are only as strong as your weakest link' – speaks volumes and is one to be recited repeatedly. The stronger the single piece, the stronger the overall chain.

Once I have the behaviour on cue, I can start building my history of reinforcement for the correct behaviour. I would do this by getting my dog to perform what Karen Pryor (author of *Don't Shoot The Dog)* refers to as 'twofers' or 'threefers'. This is a nickname for getting your dog to perform several repetitions of one behaviour for one click.

For example, three sits for one click, or two downs for one click. It is important that the behaviour stays the same, with no deterioration. In technical terms, this is referred to as a variable schedule of reinforcement (VSR). The science shows us that VSR is the way to create stronger more efficient, reliable behaviour.

LINKING BEHAVIOURS

Once you have a single behaviour on a VSR, you are ready to link it with another new behaviour, for example combining a sit and a down, or a sit and a stand. You could even bridge this stage of learning by rewarding each single behaviour with a lower level reward, for example, a pat. So the chain would be sit, (pat and fuss), down 'click'. This is a simple chain of two behaviours, strung together with praise, which could be considered a secondary reinforcer (for most dogs, unless you have one that particularly loves praise), leading to a 'click' which results in a high value reinforcer.

Now that you are linking two separate behaviours together, and reinforcing for completion of the two bits, you may wish to lower the criteria you have set for the individual behaviours and still reward for completion of the two pieces. So, if I am asking for a sit and a down, I may accept a slower down after the sit if the dog had pieced the two things together. Asking a dog to piece different behaviours together without primary reinforcement – until the two behaviours have been performed – is a huge ask for a dog that has always been reinforced for everything he does. Remember you are starting a chain of behaviour, so the chain is what you should be training and rewarding.

CREATING A CHAIN

Restrain the dog while the toy is thrown.

Send the dog.

The pick-up.

Returning with the toy.

Giving up the toy.

Your criteria for the individual pieces is going to be lowered, but not dropped altogether. You would expect at least an average performance of the single behaviour before going on to the next section.

If the performance deteriorates to the point where the individual behaviour is sub-standard, you would need to go back a step. You would need to ensure that the single behaviour has been sufficiently reinforced for exactly what you want, and that a strong history of reinforcement has been created before linking it with another behaviour.

Once you start to build a chain of behaviour, there will be two points that will convey to the dog that he has completed the sequence correctly. The most obvious will be the click and reward at the end of the sequence. The dog has completed a chain of behaviours correctly, with each behaviour performed "average or better" (a Susan Garrett saying), resulting in a click and reward.

The second indicator that tells the dog he has completed the section of the chain correctly is allowing the sequence to continue. One correct response, which has its own history of reinforcement, leads to the next behaviour, which has its own history of reinforcement and, eventually, a chain which will have a history of reinforcement all of its own! The behaviour will be self-rewarding, due to the strong association that has been built up with reinforcement.

COMPLETING THE CHAIN

Linking behaviours into a chain can seem like quite a challenge but, again, it is easy if you take it step by step.

Let's take the retrieve as an example. You have taught each behaviour separately and built up a history of reinforcement for each tiny part. You now want to link several bits together.

Initially, I would start work on a baby chain. At this stage, I don't want to put the whole exercise together as I am not happy with certain parts. Let's say, for example, I haven't got a strong sit with duration so I don't want to put this in the chain as yet. I will therefore start the exercise by restraining my dog, yet still work on the look, outrun, pick up and return. I could ask the dog to bring the article to my hand, rather then put the 'present' into the chain. This chain can be edited to suit the individual and his stage of learning.

The final stage is to complete the chain, linking all the behaviours into one sequence. So this would be the chain as required for the respective sport or criteria you have set. So for a formal retrieve in competitive obedience this would be a set up, sit, wait, outrun, pick up, return, present/front and finish.

What happens if the dog successfully completes the whole sequence but, the moment when you are going to click, the quality of the behaviour deteriorates to average?

You have two choices:

- Firstly, you could initially ignore it and still reward as you are going for the whole sequence. You would mentally make a note of the weak element and go back and train that at a separate session.
- Alternatively, you could ignore the weak response and continue on to another exercise. You would still need to work on the weakness at a separate session.

Both are feasible options.

Proofing Games

Here are a few games to play that will test your dog's ability and understanding of behaviours, chains and component parts:

1. Do one exercise out of the trained sequence.

2. Mix up the exercises in the chain.

3. Do the chain backwards.

4. Do the chain with extreme distraction.

5. Do the chain twice in a row.

6. Do one of the exercises five times for one reward.

7. Change the tone of your verbal cues.

8. Simon says: This is one of my foundation games, where I change my body language and test if my dog understands my verbal cues. For more information, see Chapter 12.

9. Change the set-up you use to test the understanding of the verbal cue.

10. Set up your dog on the other side, e.g. right as opposed to left.

HAVE FUN!

When you are working on a chain of behaviours, don't get over-awed by the magnitude of the task.

Remember that component training means that the vast majority of behaviours can be trained in under five minutes, and that once the dog is 'in the game', his speed of learning will sky rocket in trying to work out what he needs to do to earn a click!

And most important of all... have fun! If you are not having fun, the chances are your dog isn't! So... make sure you laugh a little – and go for your goals!

Chapter Eleven

CHANNELING DRIVE AND BUILDING DURATION

We have looked at how we can build drive in dogs using appropriate delivery of reinforcement. But what do we do when we get it, or if we have a dog that has drive in abundance, or even in excess? The answer is that we must learn to channel drive so that it doesn't become our enemy.

KEY FACTORS

Here is a list of key factors that will allow you to have a driven, enthusiastic dog that throws himself into the task at hand, with accuracy and commitment:

1. Clear criteria is one of the main considerations that will affect drive being an asset rather then a hindrance. Do you know exactly what you want from each behaviour? Have you ensured that the dog understands this, too?
2. Self-control, which involves teaching clear release words around play. Do you have a clear "get the toy" cue and a clear "let go of the toy" cue?
3. Playing regular self-control games, for example, Susan Garrett's *Itsyerchoice* (see page 131). The mantra 'positive is not permissive' should be a regular occurrence in your training.
4. 'Simon says' is a game where you test and challenge your dog's understanding of verbal cues regardless of your body language (see page 133).

A high drive dog gives you a competitive edge – but how do you control it.

5. Adding arousal to your training sessions. With highly driven dogs, the approach is to keep your training calm, sedate and safe. However, this gives a false illusion and does not prepare you – or him – when you are put in a situation where the state of arousal is raised. You need to add arousal in a training situation where you can work through it systematically.

6. Physical stimulation. Is your dog getting adequate outlets for his energy? Often dogs are unable to control their enthusiasm simply because they have too much pent-up energy. If this is the case, the exercise quota should be increased, or made more demanding.

7. Alternating between food and toys is a must if you want to control and channel drive. A highly-aroused, intense dog will often stop taking food or toys. If this is the case, you must immediately stop in your tracks and fix the issue (see Chapter Nine: Refining Reward and Reinforcement).

8. Work on appropriate warm up routines before competing. Getting your dog in the zone is essential, and doing the right things before you go in will have a dramatic effect on his performance when he is competing. This often takes trial and error to work out. Practise this in training, before you go to a show or trial.

9. Build duration into your behaviours. A high drive dog, who wants to live life

in the fast lane, needs to learn that this tactic does not always pay off. Teach your dog to be perfectly still, then explode off the spot, and then be perfectly still again. This is a vital part of learning control.

10. Shaping behaviour is a great way to teach your dog to work through frustration and, more importantly, to think whilst in a heightened state of arousal. But in order not to add to his frustration, you need to be specific about what you want and engineer the environment so that the dog doesn't make numerous incorrect responses and become increasingly aroused. Be specific in what you shape, and keep a crystal clear picture in your mind of what you want to achieve.

YOU'VE GOT IT – NOW MAKE IT LAST!

Capturing a behaviour is one thing, making it last is quite another. Building duration is an issue that comes into play when training all types of dogs from the high drive dog who is impatient to move on to the next task, to the less motivated dog who is inclined to bale out.

Those just starting out with crossover training often struggle to maintain or sustain duration behaviours, be it a behaviour chain or an individual behaviour. We have an overriding desire to reward our dogs, which tempts us into making behaviour chains short and easy. So for sports that require sustained behaviours, there is a high risk that the dog will fall apart in competition.

A typical pattern would be that the dog has not been adequately prepared for the duration aspect of a test. In obedience, this would be the series of exercises that comprised a complete round; in agility terms this would be completing the whole round of jumps, weaves, tunnels and contacts. In competition, a dog needs to string these individual exercises together in order to complete the round or test. This requires the dog to complete several behaviour chains in sequence, for a length of time. This may be seconds, minutes or longer. For example in the top level of Mondio, time in the ring can be up to 45 minutes. Regardless of the exact time, duration is a big ask for any dog. Under the stress of competition, the dog may become inattentive, anxious, or he may start barking.

To counteract this, the handler intervenes in some way, shape or form and, as a result, reinforces the unwanted behaviour. Before you know it, the chain of behaviour becomes shorter and shorter, or may be lost altogether.

So what do you do to avoid and overcome this issue?

BUILDING DURATION STEP-BY-STEP

The first thing is to establish the length of time your dog can sustain a simple behaviour.

So for heelwork specifically, I build duration with a moving hand touch or an exercise I call food follow. This is where my dog trots underneath my outstretched hand, similar to lunging a horse, so that I don't have to worry about the technical aspects of heelwork, my handling, or the dog's specific position on my leg.

Building duration entails teaching your dog to focus and concentrate over an extended period of time.

I take the complexities out of the equation, and just do a simple straight line, a circle, or a serpentine where I walk in one direction, without incorporating turns but, instead, moving in a series of left and right curves.

I then time the exercise in terms of the number of steps I am taking. This means determining how many 'clean' steps I can take without the dog looking away, losing commitment, or becoming inattentive.

When duration is established, and it becomes impractical to count the number of steps you are taking, you can switch to timing the exercise with a stopwatch.

When you first assess duration by counting steps, the total of clean steps you achieve will be disappointingly low. But you can build on this.

For example:
- Your dog can do 15 steps without any changes in the criteria you have set – he is performing the exercise exactly as you would want.

- Now you are going to repeat the steps, but do it in two sets of 10, with a little praise, but no reward in-between. So 10 steps –"good boy, aren't you clever" – then another 10 steps. So the dog has done less then he can do in each set (10) but more in total (20).
- Repeat this in varying sets; so the combination might be 12+8, 11+9 etc.
- When the dog is giving you 20 clean steps in two sets, aim for another 20 steps.
- If the dog initially dropped (i.e. lost focus) between 15-20 steps (so beyond his maximum duration), I would allow a recovery. This is where the dog drops but then recovers from the error. So for example, he gets to 18 steps and looks away, comes back for 2 more clean steps, which you can then reward. So at first, the dog is doing 20 steps in total – with a recovery.
- You can progress this quickly by adding more steps after the recovery. So now when the dog gets to 18 and drops, add another 7 or so before rewarding. In this way, he exceeds his previous maximum with a blip in-between.
- Continue with this, jackpotting the dog after recovery so that he wants to 'stay in the game'. In this way, you will eliminate the blip altogether.
- Be careful that duration with a blip/recovery doesn't become part of the chain! So, once you have overcome the recovery/blip stage, there should be a zero count if the dog has a blip. So the dog gets to 15 (your previous minimum) and has a blip. So now the count goes back to 0, and you start again without breaking off. This means the dog has to do 15 steps again. Remember, you need to go through the process of the dog recovering from the mistake first in order for this to be effective.

To continue building duration, keep reverting to sets. Once you have a large number revert regularly to polishing the bits and pieces to ensure criteria remains intact.

In agility terms, building duration would be where I progress my dog from being able to jump over one jump and go through a tunnel, to being able to do two jumps then a tunnel, then three jumps and a tunnel… and so forth. I can go back and forth between the maximum number to the minimum number of jumps, to build confidence and desire.

Chapter Twelve

MY FAVOURITE
FOUNDATION GAMES

If you were building a house, one of the most important parts of the process is digging the foundations. The investment, both in time and resources, is best spent on ensuring that this layer is solid and well-grounded. The same is applicable to dog training. The secret of creating a dog that can perform at the top level in any sport is to start with solid foundations.

I have developed a variety of foundation games, with both food and toys, which allow me to train any single behaviour, or exercise, in the most efficient manner possible.

You may think that playing games with your dog is a waste of time; it is true, you can train behaviours and exercises without recourse to them. However, the long term effects of neglecting this basic level of training can be costly and resource intensive.

For example, one of the foundation games I play is an informal play retrieve (see page 153). This is where the dog races out at speed, picks up a toy and returns it to hand. Now look at this in the context of agility training. You are training the weaves and you want to reinforce your dog. There are several options to consider but, ideally, you want a system that

Foundation games have an important part to play in all aspects of training.

will create fast, independent and accurate weaves. The obvious reinforcer would be to reward with a toy or to throw food. But unless you have a particularly large treat, throwing food may be difficult. Equally, if your dog doesn't have the ability to bring the toy back, you will have to keep hold of it, ask an assistant to help, or tie the toy to a long line. All these options have downsides.

The best option would be to throw the toy after the dog has completed the weaves so he can pick it up, bring it back, and then repeat the exercise. So the skill of training fast, independent weaves is actually built on a foundation of a solid informal play retrieve. This is just one example where foundation skills can have a knock-on effect as to how you train a behaviour.

BASIC SKILLS
In order to play foundation games successfully, your dog needs to acquire a basic skill set relating to both toys and food.

TOYS
Your dog needs to be able to carry out the following behaviours:
1. Tug: The dog should tug with any object that you present; the tug should be both committed and interactive. The dog should be active in the act

of tugging, and if you let go of the toy he should instantly bring it back to you to continue the game. *For information on tugging, see Chapter Five: Building Play.*

2. Value for a moving toy: The dog should pursue the toy whilst in motion; this may be thrown, moved in your hand, or activated on a line/flirtpole. *For advice on establishing play, see Chapter Five.*

3. Value for a dead toy: The dog should have value for a toy that is stationary; it may be placed be on the floor, positioned up high or from your hand. *For further information, see page 147.*

4. Release of the toy: The dog should release the toy on a verbal cue, and not touch it again until given permission.

5. Informal play retrieve (IPR): The dog runs out to retrieve a toy, turns and drives back to deliver it to the handler.

You are looking for a strong, committed, interactive tug.

The IPR includes a number of components, which can be taught separately before putting the whole exercise together. *For information on training an IPR, see page 153.*

FOOD
Skills in relation to food: These are the skills your dog needs when you are working with food as a reinforcer:

1. *Itsyerchoice:* Susan Garrett's game is a metaphor for the dog understanding that reinforcement is contingent on certain behaviours. (For step-by-step training, see page 131). Although, I start working with food, this is a concept that I apply to all aspects of the life that I lead with my dogs, and so, in time, the reinforcer may be simply verbal praise.

2. Shaping: Start shaping simple behaviours with food (see Shaping and Luring,

Chapter Two). You may progress to using a toy as a reinforcer but it is best to start with food as it creates more of a thinking state of mind in your dog.

3. Tweezer fingers: This is the ability to deliver food with fingertips pressed together like a pair of tweezers. This promotes accuracy with behaviours, and also incorporates an element of self-control.
4. Food circuits: This is a method of delivering food, which invokes prey drive. *For step-by-step training, see page 139.*
5. Name game: This is a game where food is thrown out, and the dog is allowed to chase after it. He is called back with his name, and then another piece of food is thrown in the opposite direction. *For step-by-step training, see page 141.*

Your dog should be familiar with the concept of shaping so that he builds on the behaviours that are reinforced and rewarded.

What Treats Should I Use?

When you are playing games with your dog, and using food as a reward, you want a treat that is:

- High in value
- Quick and easy to eat
- Keeps its shape – for some games you will need to throw the treat or roll it along the ground. In some cases, it helps if the treat bounces when it is thrown as this ignites a dog's prey drive.
- Is different in colour to the surface you are working on.

I find the best treats to use are hot-dog sausages, or cocktail sausages, cut into small chunks. Cheese cut into cubes can also work well.

You need to work in a location that is fairly open so you can throw your treats a reasonable distance, or as far as possible, to cause the dog to run at speed. Ideally the surface should be relatively flat. This will ensure the game flows and the dog doesn't have to hunt for the treat that has been thrown.

ITSYERCHOICE

As a professional trainer and dog sports coach, I consider the path I travel a journey of personal discovery via dog training. Along this path, there are milestones which have catapulted my thinking, training and results light years ahead. One of those biggest milestones is the concept and application of *Itsyerchoice* into my dogs' lives.

Itsyerchoice (IYC) is a principle created by my peer, mentor and friend Susan Garrett. She teaches the notion that the most effective way to live with your dog, in a reinforcement based dog-training system, is to harness what *the dog* wants to become what *you* want.

This concept goes beyond the simplicity of food and toys, and looks to the environment, our interactions, and anything else that the dog deems as

131

The dog must maintain a controlled position in order to earn the reinforcement.

reinforcing to him. By harnessing the power of the dog's desire to attain the reinforcement, and transferring the 'value' of the reinforcement to us, we create a dog that is incredibly focused, clear and driven – without the use of punishment, force or aversive methods.

The simplest variation of IYC, is to start with holding treats in your hand:

- Sit on the floor and hold some high value treats in your hand. Your dog will attempt to lick, bite, chew or access the food.
- Wait for the dog to offer a behaviour that you want, rather than the persistant mugging.
- When he does this, open your hand. He will instantly try to rush in, and grab the food. If he attempts to do this, close your hand and wait. Again repeat, as above, when the dog stops mugging.
- Repeat the above steps until the dog can hold a controlled position whilst your palm is open and the food in in sight. This is critical. Clenching your fist around the food, in an effort to stop the dog accessing the food, is a way of managing the dog's behaviour rather then teaching him to seek permission from you in order to access reinforcement. When the dog holds position, deliver the treat while keeping your palm open.
- You can grow this game to dropping food, and waiting for the dog to hold a controlled position, or throwing it, or even placing it on your foot, etc. The possibilities are endless.

This simple game is a metaphor for how we wish our dogs to see reinforcement in their environment. They can request permission to access their reinforcement by behaving or giving us behaviour that we want.

So, for example, the dog that wants to go out for a walk has to automatically sit at the gate, without a cue, as if to say 'please' can we go for a walk. If the dog opts not to sit, you would wait, hence the term – *Itsyerchoice*. When the dog makes the right choice, he is reinforced by the gate opening. If he proceeds, walking nicely on the lead, he then gets to go to the park. The reinforcement for the appropriate behaviour is the chance to do the thing the dogs wants. Once you view the world through the dog's eyes, and ask yourself the question: 'where is the reinforcement?' you can start to identify and resolve any issue that your dog has, be it a domestic issue or a sports-related issue. A dog that doesn't want to tug can be motivated to do so if he loves to swim. You can use the opportunity to swim as a reinforcement for tug.

The implementation and understanding of IYC has changed the way I live my life and, therefore, the lives my dogs lead.

SIMON SAYS

Simon Says is a simple and effective game that grows your dog's understanding and creates what I call, the 'success protocol', which can be applied to any behaviour you wish to teach. The idea of the game is that your dog is able to do a simple behaviour, like a sit, irrespective of your body position. It is therefore reliant on your dog understanding the verbal cue for the behaviour.

This is how to play:

- Allow your dog to move around in front of you. Initially start with simple body language – for example, put your hands on your head and ask your dog to "sit". If your dog goes into position, reward him and then move him off the spot.
- Now try another body position, for example: hands on shoulders and ask your dog to "sit". If he responds correctly, reward him and encourage him to move again.
- Progress the game by varying your body language. My preference is to move my hands lower on my body, so hands on hips... "sit", hands on knees... "sit", hands on shins... "sit", hands on toes..."sit".

A lot of dogs will start to miss the position once your hands get lower to the ground. This is because of conflicting body language which tempts your dog to go into a down position.

SUCCESS PROTOCOL

When you hit a point of failure, you can invoke the 'success protocol'.

Imagine your dog failing, and your response, as a two-way game between you and your dog. So if your dog fails, you can turn your response into a game between you and your dog. When he makes a mistake, 'celebrate' by laughing it off, and teasing him with the reinforcement he missed out on. Often this, in itself, can be enough to bring success when you try again.

However, if your dog makes the same mistake – repeat the 'celebration'. Failure on the dog's part should not be about 'good' or 'bad'; it isn't a judgment, it's an opportunity to enhance his knowledge. I will happily allow my dog to fail three to five times, and celebrate my victory before considering a change in what I am doing.

When discussing 'failure', there are a few key points to remember. The dog must have had a long and healthy history of reinforcement for the behaviour you are asking for. In the session you are 'creating' failure, you must have done several repetitions with the dog being successful before creating or asking any further questions. If your dog continues to fail, it's time to make the challenge easier.

However I would not go back to a stage that is too easy, as I would not be developing my dog's understanding. For example, if my dog was successful when I placed my hands on my knees and asked him to "sit", but failed when I touched my toes, I will put my hands on my shins and ask him to "sit".

If he is successful, I can jackpot him and stop, or do a simple version of the game and reward.

If your dog fails, at this slightly easier stage, again, I would make light of it and try an even easier stage. I may even repeat a simpler version, but not necessarily reinforce the dog with a high value reward. The idea of this game is to challenge your dog a little bit, so that he grows in understanding and, therefore confidence.

When your dog is successful after a struggle, make sure you have a party and then make it easier. Don't keep increasing the difficulty as this will affect his confidence. Always consider your training holistically, so, ideally, your next session should be easier and less challenging.

This process can be applied to any behaviour or skill that you want to grow, be it distance, duration or repetitions. The 'success protocol' is a concept that can help to develop your dog's understanding, while building confidence. The notion of finding the point where you dog is likely to struggle, and making it either easier or strategically challenging him, is something that is needed for all sports dogs.

Always remember, your dog's confidence is the indicator of how far to go in any given session, so use this as your guide.

HAND TOUCH

A hand touch is a great skill to teach your dog as it has several practical uses for dog sports, including teaching heelwork, retrieves, distance control and positions, not to mention its use in agility.

However, the underlying benefit of teaching a hand touch is that the dog learns the concept of 'connecting' in order to earn reinforcement. The food can be held in one hand and the dog has to touch the other to receive it. He has to process the concept of moving away from the reinforcement, or offering an alternative behaviour, to receive reinforcement. A hand target can be shaped by showing your dog your palm, and then marking him for making contact with it. When you reinforce, position the food near the hand to encourage him to focus on it. You want the dog to see the palm of the hand as a cue to drive his nose into it. You can shape him either doing individual hand targets repeatedly, or a constant, sustained hand target.

This is what to do:
- Make sure you have high value food in your hand, and create some interest in it. I pretend that I am eating it myself, as this tends to draw my dog's focus to my hands and what I have in them.
- When the dog is looking at you, present your hand – the palm facing him – at his head height. You don't want the dog needing to jump or reach for your hand; you want to keep it simple and easy.
- Out of curiosity, the dog will probably investigate your hand. As he makes

135

A hand touch has many applications, and always has the underlying benefit of bringing your dog back into contact with you.

contact with your hand with his nose, mark this behaviour and feed near the hand. I prefer not to place the food in the hand I want the dog to make contact with, as he is likely to lick it. If the dog doesn't make contact with the hand, you can shape him for showing interest, marking him for looking at it, or moving towards it, then eventually making contact with it.

- Once you have a consistent touch, you can decide whether to build duration, or to reinforce repeated touches.
- For either response, I withhold the click when he touches, and wait for him to return to the hand and offer another touch.
- The sustained hand touch is created by reinforcing the dog when he taps out a 'morse code'. This is where he repeatedly taps (or touches) as he tries to earn his reinforcer. At some point he will push more intently into your hand, or remain in contact with it. Initially this may be brief but you can mark it as a starting point to build on.
- Once the dog has been shaped to do either a sustained hand touch or repeated tapping, present both hands to the dog. One will be an open palm facing the dog, and the other will be a clenched fist with food in it. The dog has to move away from the hand holding the food and touch the opposite hand, in order to receive the food. It may help to have the clenched fist slightly further away from the dog at first, to make it easier for him.

You can progress the hand touch by introducing challenges and trying to tempt your dog away. You can also play *Itsyerchoice,* when he is in contact with your hand and test if he understands that he must remain in contact.

SPIDER HANDS

This is a simple way to engage your dog and encourage him to show interest in your hands, which will benefit your informal play retrieve (see page 153).

- Start with your dog in a quiet place so he is not distracted and engage him with a toy or with food.
- Allow him to win the toy or, if you are working with food, throw a treat a short distance. You want him at a distance from you, but not so far away from you that he wanders off. I would suggest he is no more than a metre (3 ft). If need be, play this game in an enclosed area or keep your dog on a lead.
- Casually start to move your hand as though it were a spider scurrying along the ground. You can hide your hand and then dart it out, or start to move it slowly as though creeping along the ground. You are aiming to get your dog to 'notice' your hand.
- When he shows an interest, you can either click and feed him from the hand, or interact with the toy, using the same hand. The aim of this game is to get the dog interested in your hand, and build a positive association with it.
- You can progress this by seeing if your dog will bring his toy towards your hand. Often, a dog will drop the toy and pursue the hand. If this happens, stop moving your hand, grab the toy, and tease him with it. The idea of this part of the game is that the dog wants to keep possession of the toy, or the 'spider' will grab it.
- Progress this to tugging or throwing the toy and the dog driving the toy back to your hands.

COLLAR GRABS

This game teaches your dog to accept being held and restrained by his collar or harness. It is an essential skill that allows you to play many of the following games. In agility training, it is very useful when working with restrained recalls, which are fundamental to foundation training.

- Start with your dog either playing or taking treats from your hand.
- As he is engaged with taking the treats or playing with the toy, keep touching his collar and his neck. Keep going until he is completely desentistised to your touch.
- Progress to grabbing the collar and delivering a treat at the same time. You can

also build up a position association with the collar being touched so that the dog doesn't become hand shy.

- If your dog wears a harness, you can play the same game – but touch around his shoulders and back – so that he becomes accustomed to being restrained by his harness.

RESTRAINED RECALLS

This game is useful for building drive for recalls, retrieves and scentwork. In agility, it encourages drive and forward focus. Chase is a huge natural instinct, which can create an immense amount of focus if you harness it and make yourself the chase object.

Restrained recalls can be trained either with an assistant restraining your dog, or on your own using a long line. If you are working on your own, wrap the long line round a pole, a fence or a tree, and attach it to your dog's collar. The line must run freely so it acts as a pulley.

- If you are working with a long line, you can leave your dog in a sit/down or stand. However, this game is all about building drive and speed – not self-control – in the formative stages.
- When you leave your dog, tease and bait him, but don't use his name until you are ready for him to be released.
- When you want him to come, use his name or recall cue, and allow your assistant to release him or, if he is tied, release him yourself. Initially do this whilst you are running away.
- You can progress this to building in a delay before you run off, and shape your dog driving to you by leaving it later and later before you run off.

FOOD CIRCUITS

Food circuits are brilliant for creating prey drive in dogs that are primarily motivated by food.

They are a fast and fun way to reinforce your dog, and deliver food in a different format rather than routinely giving treats. This game also encourages fast returns on retrieves and recalls.

The idea of the game is to throw the treat out and for the dog to race after it. This is what to do:

Reinforcing a collar grab allows you to work with restrained recalls, which you will need in many of my foundation games.

- Start with your dog alongside you, or restrain him by holding his collar if you prefer.
- Aim to throw the treat as far as possible, making sure the dog sees it being thrown out. In the formative stages, throw the treat underarm so it is in the dog's eye line, allowing him to follow its path of travel.
- When you throw the treat, aim to skim or bounce it so it creates motion, and keeps the dog's interest.
- If you are restraining your dog, release him to pursue the treat. I use a verbal cue to let my dog know he is free to get the treat.
- Once the dog has eaten the treat, encourage him to come back to you with a

noise or by stepping backward. Avoid using his name as you want to fade this aid within a few repetitions.

- As the dog comes back to you, show him a treat, held in your hand, and turn on the spot 360 degrees. You should now be back where you started.
- Repeat the throw out, and call him back.
- Each time you do this, fade the amount of help you give to encourage him back.
- Once the dog is in the flow of running out, eating the treat and being taken round your body, you can start to fade the extent to which you are turning. You are aiming for the dog to circle your body independently, without your assistance. The idea is to create a race-track pattern where the dog is running out, circling you and then running out again.
- You can vary this by allowing your dog to change the direction he circles you, or he can go through your legs.

CORNER THROWS

Corner throws are a great way to create really tight fast pick ups and returns with a toy, or for teaching your dog to turn quickly and tight.

You can work from a corner, or set up a barrier for this game.

Before starting, make sure your dog is comfortable with collar grabs or harness grabs. You will also need to use large, visible treats that are easy to track.

This is what to do:

- Position yourself a short distance from your corner/barrier, and restrain your dog by his collar/harness.
- Throw a treat into the corner/barrier and release your dog to get it. I use a verbal cue to give him permission to get it.
- As your dog leaves you, start to run in the opposite direction. As soon as he has got his treat, he should turn to chase after you. You may need to use a verbal cue, such as calling his name, to encourage him to chase after you. But try to fade this as quickly as possible.
- Repeat this game, and increase the distance and the delay before sending your dog to get the treat. If he loses sight of the treat, don't allow him to hunt for it. Instead, run in and pick it up. You want your dog to understand

that he has to focus on the treat or he may lose it.
- You can progress to throwing a toy into a corner and repeating the game.
- Once you have conditioned your fast, tight turn you can start to throw short of the corner/barrier so your dog learns to turn sharply in the open rather than against a corner or a barrier.

NAME GAME

The name game is a great way to teach a really fantastic name response.

In addition, it can be used as a foundation game for fast recalls, informal play retrieve (see page 153) and for a formal retrieve. It can also be used as foundation for agility body language, teaching your dog to chase after you as you move away from him.

When your dog understands the name game, you can progress it by introducing blind turns and other handling moves.

For this game you will need treats that will hold their form when thrown, ideally will roll along the ground, and that are a contrasting colour to the surface you are working on. You will need to carry treats in both hands, so having a bait bag or pockets that can be filled is a definite advantage. You will be throwing the treats, underarm, in opposite directions:
- Start with your dog in front of you. Initially you can pick which hand you wish to throw with first.
- If you imagine the face of a clock, you will be positioned in the middle and you will be aiming to throw towards 3 and 9'o clock.
- Throw your first treat in whichever direction you choose. Once the dog has left you, start to move in the opposite direction. This will mean that when the dog faces you, you will be further away from where you originally were. This should cause the dog to break into a canter or gallop.
- You can encourage your dog back with making a noise or saying a silly phrase like "pup pup", but don't introduce his name as yet.
- Once the dog has eaten the treat, and you can see he is heading back to you, mark the moment he lifts his head towards you. For ease, I would suggest using a verbal marker rather then a clicker.
- Once you have marked the 'moment' he looks back to you, say "get it" and throw a treat in the opposite direction.
- When you throw, ensure you use the arm nearest the dog. If he is on the left,

throw with your left arm, if he is on your right, throw with your right arm. This ensures he sees the line of travel the treat takes, and therefore keeps the momentum of the game going.

- Once the dog has passed your body, move in the opposite direction to encourage him to return to you at speed. Repeat as above.
- As you repeat the game, you should note that the dog is anticipating the throw and looking back a lot quicker after eating.
- When you see this happen, rather then mark this behaviour, you are now going to add his name, just before the moment he looks back. This is effectively labeling the sharp response, and head snapping back, with the dog's name. This is the response you want every time you use his name.
- Repeat as above, marking and rewarding each time you see the dog is about to turn back.
- If the dog loses sight of the thrown treat, do not encourage him to go and hunt for it as this will undermine the game.

FIVE FOR FIVE

This is a brilliant game that is designed to teach attention and focus in any location. It's really simple so I play it with puppies, or simply to get the party started. You can play it with dogs that have minimal prey drive.

It is so unobtrusive, you really can take it anywhere, and the dog can't help but be successful.

You will need:

- Treats
- Bait bag (or deep pockets)
- A timer
- Dog on a lead
- Chair to sit on

Step One

You will need five treats; make sure they are of a type that the dog can eat quickly. The name of the game is quick feeding. You will want a treat that is easy to eat, visible, and high value. Cheese or pieces of Frankfurter are great options. Choose a quiet environment that has minimal distraction. This is

The name game can be adapted to practise, and reinforce, handling moves needed in agility.

an additional challenge that you can add later on. At this stage you are simply working on duration of attention.

- Sit on your chair with your dog on a lead, so he can't wander off. Take your treats and hold them in your hand. It's not a problem if your dog is aware that you have treats in your hand, or not.
- Without saying a word, stand up and count to five (not necessarily out loud...) and feed your dog a treat on every count: one second, one treat. But rather then taking the treat from your hand and feeding him direct, take it from your hand, touch your nose with the hand holding the treat, and then feed him.
- Ideally the dog will be looking at you, not sniffing the floor. The object of the game is to feed him quickly. So if he is not engaged, don't make a huge issue of it; make a noise to get his attention and start the game.
- Once you have done this, sit down. Don't make a big deal of ending the game, just sit down passively.

Step Two

- Repeat step one, two or three times until you can see your dog anticipating that, as soon as you stand up, you are going to start to feed him.

Step Three

- Repeat as step one but this time – before you start – use a word that signals to the dog that the game is 'on'. I use 'ready'. This is going to be the cue to tell the dog that there is food on offer shortly.

Step Four

- Repeat step three, but add an 'end'/'off' signal. I use "that'll do" which tells the dog he is no longer going to be fed.

Step Five

- Continue to use five treats, but extend your time frame to 10 seconds, then to 15 seconds. You don't have to give the treats at two-second intervals. Mix it up. Now you have put your reinforcement on a variable schedule, your dog should be giving you intense attention in anticipation of being fed. Repeat as above and when you deliver one of the treats to your dog throw it away from you. You are now looking to create a desire to return to you, and give attention in order to receive further reinforcement.

Step Six

- Progress to throwing your treat and, as your dog leaves you, move to a new area. You are now extending the space where your dog gives attention. Once your dog is playing this game confidently, you can add your 'on' cue prior to standing up. The aim is that when you say "ready", your dog should be attentive for an indefinite period of time until you say "that'll do".

When you are playing this game, don't always face your dog. Work sideways on, or pretend you are talking to someone else. You are teaching the dog that he should be attentive the moment he hears the cue "ready", irrespective of what you are doing, and that he is allowed to be off duty when you tell him "that'll do".

You can progress this game applying the on and off switch to your training by asking for behaviours within the time frame the dog is 'on'. For example, "Ready"... sit, down, (treat one)... stand (treat two)... dog gives attention (treat three)... down, sit, twist (treat four)... three-second gap of attention while you focus elsewhere (treat five)... "that'll do".

AROUND A CONE

This game involves shaping your dog to circle an object. You can use any piece of equipment that will remain upright, and will allow your dog to circle it. This may be a cone, a large, half-filled water bottle, a dustbin, or a tree. If you plan to compete in agility, avoid using a pole as you don't want to create confusion with weave poles later on. My preference is to have the base of the item wide enough so that the dog doesn't have to wrap it too tightly in the early stages, especially if I am working with a puppy. This can be physically challenging and I want to ensure my dog is strong enough to perform the task. I usually start with a medium-sized cone, which I can pick up and re-position as required. Again, you will need high value, visible treats that you can roll along the ground.

You can play this game either standing up or sitting down, depending on the age of your dog and his size.

- Start by holding the cone and creating interest in it. You want to be certain that your dog will engage with it.
- When your dog is showing interest in the cone, place it on the floor. If you are standing up, the cone should be close to your feet; if you sitting down, it should be directly in front of you.
- You are looking to mark any interest the dog shows in the cone. Once you are confident that your dog is engaging with it, position him to one side of your body. You can restrain him by his collar/harness if he is accustomed to this. When your dog is focusing on the cone, release him and reinforce any movement towards it.
- Imagine the face of a clock around the cone. This will allow your placement of reinforcement to be more strategic. If the dog approaches the cone and reaches the point of 3 o'clock, reinforce him further around the path that you want him to travel. So if your dog reaches 3 o'clock – and he is travelling anti-clockwise – reinforce him at 1 o'clock. You can mark the dog for reaching 3 o'clock, but

Teaching your dog to wrap a cone encourages tight turns and independence.

the reinforcement (food or toy) comes at 1'o clock. Ideally this will be rolled or thrown on the floor so that the movement encourages the dog to travel at speed around the cone.

- As your dog learns to go further around the cone, repeat this sequence of marking him for moving around the cone and reinforcing him further around.
- Once the dog is moving around the cone, withhold your marker word and wait for the dog to move even further around the cone.
- The aim is for your dog to complete a single rotation around the cone and then, if you want, you can teach him to circle the cone continually.
- Once your dog has a good understanding with one direction, you can change his start position so he can work in the opposite direction.
- At this point you are still standing close to the cone, and you are manipulating your dog's options with your body. The next stage is to gradually move further away from the cone so your dog is working independently.
- You can ask for more speed and drive by adding distance and motion with your reinforcement. Running away and letting the dog chase you, after he has circled the cone, will also help to create speed.

You can choose whether to have different cues for different directions or one verbal cue, and allow your body position to dictate the direction.

VALUE FOR A DEAD TOY

Teaching your dog to drive to a toy that is stationary, i.e. 'dead' rather than active, is a great skill that allows you to train numerous behaviours. This is a simple skill, but often overlooked. The aim is to train your dog to have intense desire to focus on and grab the toy, even though it is not moving.

You want your dog to drive to his toy even though it is 'dead'.   **Photo: Lois Morris**

- Start with a toy that your dog likes; my preference is to use a toy with a handle. Sit on the floor and engage your dog with the toy. You want to create interest in it so I use some movement, or play tug if your dog has this skill.
- Without using a cue to release the toy, take it from your dog and incorporate this into the game. Try to 'wrestle' the toy from him; this will build drive and excitement, therefore creating more intensity.
- Once you have the toy, grab your dog's collar/harness. Be mindful that this should be trained and counter conditioned prior to this game.
- Now tease the dog with the toy. Hold the dog back from getting to the toy, and move it around to create interest in it.
- Initially I only do this for a few seconds, at most, before releasing the dog. At this stage, I keep the toy in motion.
- Repeat the above stage but, this time, keep the toy still for a moment before releasing the dog. The timing of this is crucial; you should be aiming to release him when he is focusing on the toy and is still intent on getting it. As the dog is about to reach the toy, move it again. So, for a brief moment, he sees the toy stationary as he is pursuing it.
- Progress this by adding duration to the time-lapse between the toy being stationary and the dog being released.
- The final stage is to fade your hand. Simply place the toy on the floor and

remove all contact from it. As the dog approaches the toy you can either allow him to grab it whilst it remains static, or grab it just before he does and move it again. Vary between these two things until your dog is intent on the static toy, without your involvement.

- You can then repeat this game standing up, and eventually create more distance from the toy. It may help to have a toy with a longer handle, or one that sits proud from the ground. You can also race the dog to the toy, and sometimes beat him to it, which is a great way to build value and drive for a dead toy.

TOY SWAPS

With this game, you are teaching your dog to swap one toy for another, or go from one tug to another. This skill, in itself, can be grown into an informal play retrieve (see page 153) .

In addition, it creates drive on the return of retrieves and scentwork, or even a recall.

- Start by getting your dog engaged in a game of tug, and have another toy in your opposite hand.
- Make the first toy go still, by jamming it against your leg, kneeling on it, or simply stop engaging with it.
- Then ask your dog to swap for a second toy of the same value, using a verbal cue and a hand signal to instigate this. The cue is important later on as you want him to understand that he does not let go unless you give permission.
- Make the second toy active so that the dog grabs it and engages in tug with this toy.
- Repeat this in the opposite direction, so he can alternate between toys. The aim is for the dog to release the toy he is tugging, drive to the second toy, and then return to you. Don't rush in and grab the second toy as soon as your dog takes hold of it. Allow him to possess the toy and touch him somewhere on his body 8-10 times, before engaging with the toy.

TOP TIP
If you touch, or try to get hold of, the 'second' toy too quickly, you are endorsing the dog's belief that you are in opposition to him and that

you plan to 'steal' it from him. Remember, your dog instinctively wants to possess the toy rather then interact with it. The interaction part has to be trained.

So if your dog drives past you with the toy, encourage him to come in to you, or just to be near you. You could allow him to possess it for a time, then move closer gradually, and make contact with him – not with the toy. This is key: don't touch the toy.

Hopefully, the dog will edge closer and, again, you should touch his body, and not the toy. He may come in for some physical contact but he may deliberately turn away to keep the toy out of reach. No problem... take the opportunity to fuss and cuddle him. Progress this to moving away from your dog as he tries to pursue you.

This is a great game for keeping the balance between reinforcement that is away from you and reinforcement coming from you.

OUT WITH IT!

In dog training circles, releasing a toy is known as the 'out'. It is a key lesson in teaching your dog to let go on cue, and will be needed when you are working on an informal play retrieve. Teaching the out is best left until you have a strong tug, or a definite basic tug.

There are two effective methods of teaching the out: the 'swap' or the 'lock up'.

THE SWAP

The swap can be taught using an equal, or higher level reinforcement to swap for your tug. This can involve swapping to another toy (see page 153), or you may find it easier to use food.

- Engage your dog with the tug in one hand, but try not to get him over-aroused at this stage. In your other hand, hold a high value piece of food.
- Say your release cue, "out", and – a nano second later – put the food on the dog's nose.
- As he spits out the toy to get the food, mark and reward. Alternatively, you can scatter a handful of food on the ground as you say "out". Don't be subtle about showing the food; make sure your dog knows you have a high level reward on offer.

- Progress to waiting longer between the time your dog drops the toy and producing the food.
- Vary rewarding with food, allowing the dog to bite the tug again, or throw the toy as a reward.
- Add arousal and then wait for a 'please' behaviour to re-engage. For example, your dog might back away from the reward, give eye contact, or may go into a sit or a down. He should be saying: "please may I?" rather than: "give it to me now!"

THE LOCK UP

- Engage your dog in tug, but don't get let him get too aroused at this stage.
- When you want to instigate a release, bend at the waist and jam your elbows against your knees. This will 'block' you from being able to move and you will 'lock up'. The key is not to move.
- The dog will get frustrated and try to instigate the game. Brace yourself and wait.
- When the dog eventually releases, mark the behaviour and tug again.
- When your dog can read the lock up, add your verbal cue.
- Progress to adding arousal and fading the lock up.

Both methods are effective, and both have their advantages and disadvantages.

MAINTAINING THE OUT

Often dogs that are trained to re-bite after the out, i.e. they are cued to release the toy and reinforced by being given permission to bite it again, lose the behaviour as they subtly change the criteria and shape their owners to mark them. I want to train a behaviour where the dog is asking permission to bite, rather than demanding it.

Training the out effectively, and maintaining it, is similar to training a '2 on 2 off' contact in agility.

Often a dog will start to miss his contacts because he has started to alter criteria. This may be because he considers what he has to do is too simple. But in competition, the repetition of quick releases essentially waters down criteria. Training a nose touch – where the dog touches a small disc at the

Find a high-value reward to encourage the 'out'.

foot of the contact – ensures that the dog has a distinct behaviour to perform before he is released. Even in competition, if this erodes or breaks downs, the performance will still be maintained.

This principle applies to the out. You need to ask for a behaviour that requires the dog to do that bit extra in order to get permission to bite again. Personally, I like my dogs to retract from the toy. This may mean taking a few steps backwards, or performing a sit, or a down. It can be any behaviour the dog has to perform which is obvious to the handler.

Adding arousal will also be an entity that you need to proof against. Again, this is likely to cause your dog to lose the out.

When this happens (and if you build your tug appropriately, it definitely will as your dog will value the tug more and more), you will need to use a collar grab to prevent him from tugging. Collar grabs are a foundation exercise that can be introduced at any time, and specifically in the name game (see page 141).

Dealing With No Outs

If your dog will not co-operate with the out, here are a few possible causes and solutions:

1. Often no outs are caused by the handler still applying pressure to the tug. It could be subtle tension but it may be enough for the dog to think the game is still 'on' and therefore he will not let go. Ensure that you are totally passive, or kill the game by jamming your elbows against your knees, as the lock up method (see page 150), or wedge them against your body.

2. Use a collar grab (see page 138) to draw the dog against your leg. There should be no pressure on the collar, or tension. You are merely ensuring the dog cannot tug. When he eventually lets go, wait for a 'please' behaviour and then reward.

3. Re-bites and not being aware of the dog changing criteria.

4. Often letting go of the tug can kill the game. Let go and sit on the floor. When the dog chooses to offer a behaviour that you like, pick up the tug. If he comes back, drop the tug again until he understands that he has to display self-control in order to start the game again.

5. Ask a helper to hold your dog on-lead, and then walk off and have a party for one. This is stronger than a time out, and should only be used on very confident, social dogs. Remember, the helper should not engage with the dog.

BUILDING TOY SWAPS INTO AN IPR

Once you have worked on the 'out', you can incorporate it with a toy swap in preparation for an informal play retrieve.

Proceed as follows:

- Play the toy swap game (see page 148).
- When your dog has warmed up with this game, rather then deaden the first toy, let it go.
- As you let go, move in the opposite direction and activate the second toy.
- As the dog releases the first toy and comes towards you, play with the second toy.
- Casually pick up the first toy, while the dog continues to tug on the second toy.
- Let go of the second toy, move in the opposite direction, and allow the dog to re-bite the first toy.
- Work on this until the dog is letting go of whichever toy you have and engaging with the toy you activate.
- When you can see this occurring, let the toy go, and wait for the dog to look at you before activating the second toy.
- Progress this to shaping the dog to travel towards you with the first toy before activating the new toy.
- Move this on until the dog is returning with the active toy and spitting it out to get the 'new' toy'.

Often a dog will get stuck at the point where he leaves the toy behind, rather than bringing it back. If this happens, stop and wait for the dog to pick up the toy again, or race out and grab it. This should encourage the dog to keep hold of the toy and return with it, to you.

INFORMAL PLAY RETRIEVE

The informal play retrieve (IPR) is a key skill, and I spend a considerable amount of time working on it. It is not an 'obedience' exercise per se; it's more like a series of games that are linked together. The dog has to race out, grab the toy and tear back to deliver it. The dog should ideally deliver the toy to your hand, and persist in doing so even if you don't instantly take it from him.

An informal play retrieve is invaluable for anyone intending to compete in dog sports as it incorporates so many different elements – drive, control, precision and co-operation – as well as improving your relationship, and your connection with your dog. It can be created even if your dog doesn't have intense desire for a toy, and with the right reinforcement you can actually build motivation.

For me, the benefits of an IPR cannot be over-estimated. It will save you countless hours of training time, it allows you to teach new behaviours faster and more efficiently and – best of all – you can have fun at the same time!

Often young dogs and puppies do not naturally 'retrieve' toys, so this needs to be taught. Even if your dog is a natural retriever, he will need to be educated so he performs the skill in a certain manner. When I train an IPR, I want the dog to be restrained via a collar grab, or held in a controlled position, while the object is thrown. The dog marks the fall of the object and, on cue, races out in a straight line to pick it up. He then performs a 'swimmer's turn', returns at the same speed, and delivers the object to hand. In this way he is learning and rehearsing vital skills that are required for all dog sports.

These include:
• Running and turning sharply
• Changing direction at speed
• Body awareness and control
• Weight shifting
• Self-control

It also helps me to reinforce my dog at a distance and allows me to practise delivering my reinforcement efficiently and promptly so that I can move on to another repetition.

Initially, it is quite common for puppies and young dogs to want to possess the toy and not bring it back. In this situation, the youngster will often do what I call a 'drive by'. This is where he appears to be heading towards you but then veers off at the last second... highly amusing but somewhat frustrating! This is perfectly normal – in fact, it is a great thing if a dog wants to possess the toy!

The underlying behaviour to create an IPR is tugging (see Chapter Five:

Building Play). I want this to come from the dog as it builds value for him wanting to interact with me.

However, if you work at swapping toys, you will create a scenario where the dog relishes the idea of playing with you rather than taking the toy off to play with it on his own. My aim is to create a dog who prefers to be engaged with me rather than leaving me. This is a huge part of building a relationship that goes beyond the toy and the reinforcement. I want a dog that values his toy – but values it even more highly when I am involved in the game.

IPR COMPONENTS

The IPR is made up of several components, all of which can be trained with, or without, the use of a toy. This means that you don't have to have a great tug before you can start teaching elements of the exercise.

The components for IPR are as follows:
1. Collar grab and/or sit wait
2. Look forward/mark article being thrown
3. Straight outrun
4. Swimmer's turn
5. Straight return
6. Deliver to handler/letting go

1. Collar grab/sit wait
The collar grab can be trained away from the IPR to give the dog confidence and and understanding (see page 138). When your dog is happy with the collar grab, you can add some control with a sit and, eventually, a wait.

2. Look forward/mark article being thrown
You can start this with food by restraining your dog and throwing a highly visible treat for him, such as a piece of sausage. When he sees it fall, mark the 'look' and release him to the food. You can increase the time the dog holds his gaze, before allowing him to get the food. This exercise also encourages forward focus, which is an essential ingredient in agility.

Play the following games to enhance this skill:
• Name game (see page 141).

155

INFORMAL PLAY RETRIEVE

An informal play retrieve teaches so many skills
that can be applied across the disciplines.

- Food circuits (see page 139).
- Corner throws (see page 140).

3. Fast, straight outrun

This can best be achieved by exploiting a dog's desire to chase. For some dogs this comes naturally, others need to be motivated in order to

build confidence and increase speed. This exercise is valuable for agility, particularly with start line training.

Play the following games to promote a fast outrun:
- Restrained recalls (see page 138).
- Food circuits (see page 139).
- Name game (see page 141).

4. Swimmer's turn

All dog sports require the dog to run at speed and change direction at some point, and being able to practise and improve this away from the exercise itself is a huge asset. When your dog runs out to retrieve his toy, he must make a tight turn – which I call a swimmer's turn – as he changes direction to come back to you.

Play the following games to enhance this skill:

- Name game (see page 141).
- Food circuits (see page 139).
- Corner throws (see page 140).
- Zig zag chases, when your dog will chase after you as you move in a zig zag motion away from him.
- Spin/twist, where your dog will turn in a circle in either a clockwise or anti-clockwise motion.

5. Fast, straight return

This demands the same skills that are required for the outrun. It creates a dog that wants to drive to you at speed in anticipation of the amazing reinforcement coming to him. You can use a harness or flat collar and long line to practise restrained recalls, without the need for a helper, by wrapping or threading the long line around a fence post or pole and allowing it to act like a pulley.

Play the following games:

- Food circuits (see page 139).
- Name game (see page 141).
- Restrained recalls (see page 138).
- Send around a cone (see page 145).
- Value for a dead toy (see page 147).
- Toy swaps (see page 148).

6. Deliver to handler/letting go

The last part of an IPR is for the dog to deliver the toy and to let go of it quickly and willingly. Initial training involves using a hand target, which can be shaped by holding out the palm of your hand and marking the dog for

Foundation training is great for teaching skills but, even more importantly, it helps to develop and grow your relationship with your dog.

making contact. Play the following games to teach your dog to give up his toy quickly and willingly:
• Hand touch (see page 135).
• Toy swaps (see page 148).
• Releasing the toy (see page 150).

SIGNING OFF

The biggest mistake a trainer can make is rushing through foundation training in order to get to the more 'interesting' bits, which usually means focusing on their chosen discipline. However, if you lay strong foundations and teach core skills, you will save yourself immeasurable time in the long run.

This is a period of relationship building and unpressurised learning; you will be laying a solid foundation which will enable you to reap the benefits for a lifetime.

Appendix

FURTHER READING AND INFORMATION

Susan Garrett
For information on books, DVDs and e-courses, contact www.susangarrett.com
Her products are available in the UK from www.performancedog.co.uk
including:
- *Crate Games DVD*
- *Success With One Jump DVD*
- *2x2 Weave Training DVD*
- *Shaping Success*
- *Ruff Love*

Karen Pryor
Contact Karen Pryor Academy www.karenpryoracademy.com
Her best-selling book *Don't Shoot the Dog* is also available from www.performancedog.co.uk